Pass **ECDL4**

Module 5: Database

Using Microsoft Access 2003

F.R. Heathcote

Published by

PAYNE-GALLWAY
P U B L I S H E R S L T D

26-28 Northgate Street, Ipswich IP1 3DB
Tel: 01473 251097 Fax: 01473 232758

www.payne-gallway.co.uk

Acknowledgements

Every effort has been made to contact copyright owners of material published in this book. We would be glad to hear from unacknowledged sources at the earliest opportunity.

Cover design by Direction Advertising and Design Ltd

First Edition 2004

Reprinted September 2004

A catalogue entry for this book is available from the British Library.

ISBN 1 904467 33 4

Copyright © F. R. Heathcote 2004

The ECDL Trade Mark is the registered trade mark of The European Computer Driving Licence Foundation Limited in Ireland and other countries.

This ECDL Foundation approved courseware product incorporates learning reinforcement exercises. These exercises are included to help the candidate in their training for the ECDL. The exercises included in this courseware product are not ECDL certification tests and should not be construed in any way as ECDL certification tests. For information about Authorised ECDL Test Centres in different National Territories please refer to the ECDL Foundation web site at www.ecdl.com

All rights reserved

Printed in Malta by Gutenberg Press

Disclaimer

"European Computer Driving Licence" and ECDL and Stars device are registered trade marks of The European Computer Driving Licence Foundation Limited in Ireland and other countries. Payne-Gallway Publishers is an independent entity from The European Computer Driving Licence Foundation Limited, and not affiliated with The European Computer Driving Licence Foundation Limited in any manner. Pass ECDL4 Module 5 may be used in assisting students to prepare for the ECDL Module 5 examination. Neither The European Computer Driving Licence Foundation Limited nor Payne-Gallway Publishers warrants that the use of this book (Pass ECDL4 Module 5) will ensure passing the ECDL Module 5 examination. Use of the ECDL-F Approved Courseware Logo on this product signifies that it has been independently reviewed and approved by ECDL-F as complying with the following standards:

Acceptable coverage of all courseware content related to the ECDL Version 4.0.

This courseware material has not been reviewed for technical accuracy and does not guarantee that the end user will pass the ECDL Module 5 examination. Any and all assessment items and/or performance based exercises contained in this book (Pass ECDL4 Module 5) relate solely to this book and do not constitute or imply certification by The European Driving Licence Foundation in respect of any ECDL examination. For details on sitting ECDL examinations in your country please contact your country's National ECDL/ICDL designated Licensee or visit The European Computer Driving Licence Foundation Limited web site at http://www.ecdl.com.

Candidates using this courseware material should have a valid ECDL/ICDL Skills Card. Without such a Skills Card, no ECDL/ICDL Examinations can be taken and no ECDL/ICDL certificate, nor any other form of recognition, can be given to the candidate.

ECDL/ICDL Skills Cards may be obtained from any Approved ECDL/ICDL Test Centre or from your country's National ECDL/ICDL designated Licensee.

References to the European Computer Driving Licence (ECDL) include the International Computer Driving Licence (ICDL). Version 4.0 is published as the official syllabus for use within the European Computer Driving Licence (ECDL) and International Computer Driving Licence (ICDL) certification programme.

Preface

Who is this book for?

This book is suitable for anyone studying for ECDL Version 4.0 (Module 5), either at school, adult class or at home. It is suitable for complete beginners or those with some prior experience, and takes the learner step-by-step from the very basics to the point where they will feel confident using Microsoft Access to create a database and perform tasks such as querying the database, sorting and filtering information, creating input forms and printing reports.

The approach

The approach is very much one of "learning by doing". Each module is divided into a number of chapters which correspond to one lesson. The student is guided step-by-step through a practical task at the computer, with numerous screenshots to show exactly what should be on their screen at each stage. Each individual in a class can proceed at their own pace, with little or no help from a teacher. At the end of most chapters there are exercises which provide invaluable practice. By the time a student has completed the module, every aspect of the ECDL syllabus will have been covered.

Software used

The instructions and screenshots are based on a PC running Microsoft Windows XP and Microsoft Access 2003. However, it will be relatively easy to adapt the instructions for use with other versions of Access.

Extra resources

Answers to practice exercises and other useful supporting material can be found on the publisher's web site www.payne-gallway.co.uk/ecdl.

About ECDL

The European Computer Driving Licence (ECDL) is the European-wide qualification enabling people to demonstrate their competence in computer skills. Candidates must study and pass the test for each of the seven modules listed below before they are awarded an ECDL certificate. The ECDL tests must be undertaken at an accredited test centre. For more details of ECDL tests and test centres, visit the ECDL web site www.ecdl.com.

Module 1: Concepts of Information Technology

Module 2: Using the Computer and Managing Files

Module 3: Word Processing

Module 4: Spreadsheets

Module 5: Database

Module 6: Presentation

Module 7: Information and Communication

Module 5

Database

In this module you will learn some of the main concepts of databases and how to use a database on a computer. You will learn how to:

- create and modify tables
- create and modify queries
- create and modify forms
- create and modify reports
- relate tables
- retrieve and manipulate information using queries
- retrieve and manipulate information using sort tools

Module **5** Table of Contents

Introduction to Databases

What is Microsoft Access?

Microsoft Access is one of the most widely used **database packages**. Databases are used to store large amounts of information, and allow you to sort and filter the information or **data** to provide useful reports.

A database is based on **tables** of data, and each **table** contains many **fields**.

This is an example of how an art collection might look in a table of data:

Name of Painting	Artist	Gallery
Acuminatus	Mark Johnston	CCA Galleries
The North Unfolds	Neil Canning	Martin Tinney Gallery
Heat of the Day	Claire Blois	Kilmorack Gallery
Two Birches	James Hawkins	Rhue Studio

- ◉ How many **rows** are there in the table?
- ◉ How many **columns** are there in the table?

Answers:

- ❶ There are **3** columns. The column headings are the **fields**, so there are **3** fields in the table.
- ❶ There are **4** rows. The rows are the **records**, so there are **4** records in this table.

Each time the art collector purchases a new painting, he can catalogue it by adding a **new record** to the table.

The art collector can use the database to find out information such as:

- Whether he owns a particular painting
- Which paintings he owns by Neil Canning
- Which gallery a particular painting came from
- How many paintings he has from a particular gallery
- The artist of a particular painting

Databases are not often used for such small amounts of data, because the answers to the above questions can be easily answered just by looking at the table. However, if a gallery had thousands of paintings there would be thousands of rows, and the table would be so big it would take hours to answer the questions. This is where a database becomes very useful.

Before creating a database on the computer it is important to **plan** your database.

Planning a database

When planning a database you need to think about the answers to these questions:

- What is the purpose of the database?
- What information will you want to look up in the database?
- What data will you store in the database?

Letting Agency Database

During the course of this module you'll build up a database for a letting agency, **Hemlets Ltd**. Hemlets rents properties on behalf of private landlords in Ipswich. Hemlets needs the database to store information about the properties it manages and the landlords it deals with.

Purpose of the database

The staff at Hemlets need to be able to find out quickly and easily:

- Which properties are available to let
- How many bedrooms each property has
- Which properties are available for a particular monthly rent
- Whether a property is a flat, terraced, semi-detached or detached
- If the property is let, when the lease runs out
- Who is the landlord of a particular property
- Contact details of a particular landlord

Each property is owned by just **one** landlord. Each landlord may own **one or more** properties.

Your database should contain details on each property and each landlord. The next step is to decide which **fields** you need.

Based on the information given above, the table must contain the following information about each property:

- ❶ Style (flat, terraced, semi, detached)
- ❶ Bedrooms (1, 2, 3, 4, 5, or 6)
- ❶ Rent (monthly)
- ❶ Rented? (Y/N)
- ❶ Lease expiry date
- ❶ Landlord name

In addition, the following information needs to be held about each landlord:

- ❶ Title
- ❶ Initials
- ❶ Surname
- ❶ Contact number

Each of these pieces of information will be held in one **field** in your table.

Tip:

Remember that the fields in the table are the column headings.

A flat file database

A **flat file** database is a database with just **one table** in it. If the **Hemlets** database was designed as a **flat file** database, the table of data would look something like this:

PropertyRef	Style	Bedrooms	Rent	Rented	Lease Expiry	Landlord Title	Landlord Initials	Landlord Surname	Contact No
P1	Semi	3	800	Y	1/6/2003	Mrs	J	Welsh	01474 276499
P2	Flat	2	650	Y	5/12/2003	Mr	S	Hemmings	01474 572772
P3	Detached	4	1050	N		Mr	S	Hemmings	01474 572772
P4	Terraced	2	700	Y	15/8/2003	Mr	S	Hemmings	01474 572772
P5	Semi	3	850	N		Mr	M	Jenkins	01474 387465
etc..									

Tip:

The **PropertyRef** field has been added because we need one field in each record that is unique. This will be explained in more detail later.

Problems with a flat file database

It is a common problem with many flat file databases that the same data is duplicated several times. To explain why, we'll look at the example of the property table above.

Look at the different landlords who own the various properties; notice that **Mr S Hemmings** owns **three** of the properties. This means that the information for **Mr Hemmings** had to be entered **three** different times, and if he changed his telephone number, you would have to be careful to change it in all **three** rows of the table, for every property he owns.

This is not only a waste of time, but it can introduce a lot of errors in a database. It would be easy to make a spelling mistake when entering Mr Hemmings' details, for example entering **Hennings** instead of **Hemmings**. If Hemlets searched to see which properties were owned by Mr **Hemmings**, the one with the spelling mistake wouldn't be listed, and the staff at Hemlets would be none the wiser.

A relational database

The solution to these problems is to hold the data in separate tables. We need a table for the **properties** and a different table for the **landlords**. The two tables will need to be linked. A database that contains two or more linked tables is called a **relational database**. Before you learn how to design this sort of database you need to learn some new vocabulary.

An **entity** is a person or thing about which data is held. In our example there are two entities, **Property** and **Landlord**.

An **attribute** is a piece of information about the entity. For example the attributes belonging to the entity **Landlord** are **Title**, **Initials**, **Surname** and **ContactNo**.

Question: What attributes belong to the entity **Property** shown in the table above?

Answer: **PropertyRef, Style, Bedrooms, Rent, Rented** and **Lease Expiry**. There is also one other attribute – **Landlord**. (We will need to know who the property belongs to.)

Relationships

There are three different types of relationship between entities:

One-to-one   e.g. Husband and wife. A husband can have **one** wife and a wife can have **one** husband.

One-to-many   e.g. Football team and player. A football team has **many** players, but a player belongs to only **one** team.

Many-to-many   e.g. Student and subject. A student studies **many** subjects and a subject is studied by **many** students.

Question: Which of these relationships applies to **Landlord** and **Property** in the example above?

Answer: **One-to-many**: A property is owned by **one** landlord, but a landlord can own **many** properties.

Entity–relationship diagrams

Each of these relationships can be shown in an **Entity-Relationship** (E-R) diagram, as shown below:

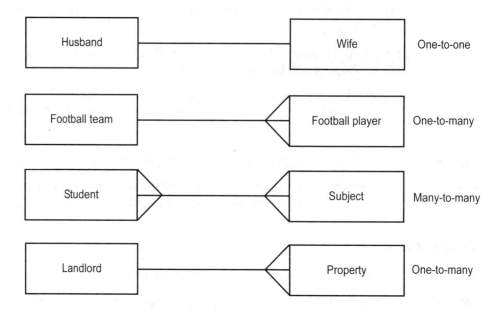

The primary key

Each entity needs its own table containing its own attributes. In addition each record in a table must have a field which uniquely identifies that record, the **primary key**.

We will use **PropertyRef** as the key field for the **Property** table. Each landlord will also be given a unique reference number, **LandlordRef**, which we can use as the key field for the **Landlord** table. We can't use **Surname** as the key field because there may be more than one landlord with the same surname.

Don't forget – although we will put the landlords' details in a separate table, we still need to know which landlord owns which property. For this, all we need to do is have an extra field in the **Property** table that contains the **LandlordRef** of the landlord who owns the property.

Now the two tables look like this:

Property table

PropertyRef	Style	Bedrooms	Rent	Rented	LeaseExpiry	LandlordRef
P1	Semi	3	800	Y	1/6/2003	L1
P2	Flat	2	650	Y	5/12/2003	L2
P3	Detached	4	1050	N		L2
P4	Terraced	2	700	Y	15/8/2003	L2
P5	Semi	3	850	N		L3
P6	Detached	5	1200	Y	25/7/2003	L4
P7	Flat	1	500	N		L5
P8	Flat	2	600	N		L5
P9	Terraced	3	750	Y	3/9/2003	L5
P10	Semi	3	900	N		L6

Landlord table

LandlordRef	Title	Initials	Surname	ContactNo
L1	Mrs	J	Welsh	01474 276499
L2	Mr	S	Hemmings	01474 572772
L3	Mr	M	Jenkins	01474 387465
L4	Mr	M	Stevenson	01474 783748
L5	Miss	L	Vacher	01474 583689
L6	Mrs	J	Hemmings	01474 856683

Question

From the two tables above, find the name of the landlord of property P7.

Answer

From the **Property** table you can see it's owned by the landlord with **LandlordRef L5**. The **Landlord** table shows that Landlord **L5** is **Miss L Vacher**.

Data types

Before you can enter these **fields** into your database, you need to think about what **format** the data will be in. Access has many different **data types**, which are explained in the table below:

Text	Letters, symbols and numbers, i.e. Alphanumeric data.
Number	Numbers only (no letters). Includes numbers with decimal points.
Date/Time	Dates and times.
Currency	For all monetary data. Access will insert a currency symbol before the amount (such as £ or $, etc.)
Yes/No	Used wherever the field can be one of only 2 values, Y/N, True/False, Male/Female etc.
AutoNumber	This is a unique value generated by Access for each record.

You will have to choose a data type for each field from the table given above. For example, should you hold a telephone number as a **Text** field or a **Number** field? At first you may think that a **Number** field would be best but in practice this is a bad idea for two reasons:

❶ Access will not record leading zeros in a number field. So if the telephone number is **01473874512** it will be recorded as **1473874512** which is incorrect.

❶ Access will not allow you to put a space, bracket or hyphen in a number field. Therefore, you should use a text field for a telephone number or you will not be able to record it as, for example, **01473 874512**.

Field properties

When you enter the field names used in each table into Access, you can specify the field length for **Text** fields. This means that Access won't create excessively large fields when you create forms and other database objects. It can also act as a type of **data validation**, as Access won't let you enter anything in a field that has more characters than the specified field length.

For **Date/Time** fields you can specify the format of the date (e.g. **dd/mm/yy** or **mm/dd/yy** etc.).

For **Currency** fields you can specify the number of decimal places.

The database structure

The **structure** of the database can be thought of as what the table will look like without any information in (i.e. the design of the table). To describe the structure you need to know:

❶ How many **fields** the table will have (the columns in the table)

❶ What the **field names** will be (the column headings)

❶ What **data type** will be held in each field

The number of rows will change as the user enters more data, and is not part of the database structure.

It is important to know the difference between the **database structure** (think of the empty table) and the **data** held in the database (the information that you put into the table).

Questions:

For each of the following changes to the **Painting** database on Page 5-1, would you need to change the database structure or edit the data?

You decide to add a new field name, **Price**, to the database.

The painting **Two Birches** was actually purchased from **Kilmorack Gallery**.

Answers:

If you add a new field name, you are changing the database structure.

If you are changing the **Two Birches** record, you are only editing the data.

Naming conventions

We will use a common convention when naming tables and fields. This means putting **tbl** in front of the table names, and not using any spaces in any of the names. Use capital letters in the middle of a field name to make the words easier to read. Look at the table below to see examples:

tblProperty

Field Name	Data Type	Field Length/Type
PropertyRef	AutoNumber	
Style	Text	15
Bedrooms	Number	Long Integer
Rent	Currency	0 decimal places
Rented	Y/N	-
LeaseExpiry	Date/Time	-
LandlordRef	Text	4

tblLandlord

Field Name	Data Type	Field Length/Type
LandlordRef	Text	4
Title	Text	4
Initials	Text	4
Surname	Text	20
ContactNo	Text	15

This will be the structure of the **tblProperty** and **tblLandlord** tables.

Notice that **PropertyRef** and **LandlordRef** have been underlined; this is because they are both primary keys.

In text fields, you should set the field length to be the length of the longest word you expect to be entered. We wouldn't expect a **Surname** to be longer than 20 letters.

Exercises

1. A library wants to keep a database to record the books borrowed by library users. Each library user has their own unique ID, and can take out up to 6 books at a time. Each book has its own unique book number. The database designer has decided that three tables will be needed, called BOOK, LIBRARY-USER and LOAN. The LOAN table will hold details of who has which books out on loan. Once a book is returned to the library, the loan record is deleted, so that there is never more than one loan record in the LOAN table for a given book.

    (a) What is the relationship between BOOK and LOAN?

    (b) What is the relationship between LIBRARY-USER and LOAN?
         Label the following entity-relationship diagram.

    (c) What is an attribute?

2. A school database is to be constructed to help the school keep track of who has been entered for each examination. Each student may be entered for several examinations.

   (a) Name two entities in the database. Suggest a primary key for each entity.

   (b) What is the relationship between the two entities?

3. A hospital database is to hold details of which patients and which nursing staff are assigned to each ward. Each nurse may be assigned to a single ward, but each ward may have several nurses. A patient is assigned to a single ward.

   (a) What is the relationship between WARD and PATIENT?

   (b) Name one other entity in this database.

   (c) Design the structure of each of the WARD and PATIENT tables. Show suitable field names. Show data types and field lengths for each field.

   (d) Make up three data records for each table.

4. A Sports Competition database is created showing all the competitors and events, and who entered which event. Some of the data is shown below:

COMPETITOR

CompetitorID	Surname	Firstname	Date of Birth	Sex
C1	Grand	Jane	01/04/84	F
C2	Keino	Michael	14/02/85	M
C3	Dowsett	Robert	12/04/84	M
C4	Perez	Juanita	31/07/85	F

EVENT

EventID	EventName	Men/Women
E1	Long Jump	M
E2	Long Jump	W
E3	100M	M
E4	100M	W
E5	100M Hurdles	M

Michael Keino entered Long Jump and 100M Hurdles (Men)

Robert Dowsett entered the 100M race (Men).

Jane Grand and Juanita Perez entered the 100M race (Women).

Fill in the data in table EVENT-ENTRY. (The column headings are given below):

EVENT-ENTRY

EventID	CompetitorID
...	...

CHAPTER 5.2

Creating a New Database

Over the next several chapters you will be creating and developing the **Hemlets** database.

Opening Access

You can open Access in one of two ways:

- ◐ *Either* double-click the **Access** icon on the main screen in Windows
- ◐ *Or* click the **Start** button at the bottom left of the screen, then click **Programs**, then click

Your screen will look like the one below:

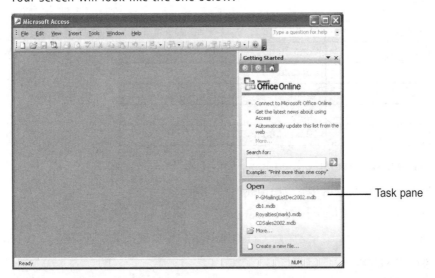

Task pane

Tip:
Your screen may look different if you have a different version of Access. If so, check the **Blank Access Database** button and click **OK**.

You now have the option of either opening an existing database or creating a new one. We will create a new database from scratch.

◉   Click **Blank Database** in the Task pane.

A window opens similar to the one shown below, asking you to select a folder and a name for your new database.

◉   Click the **Create New Folder** button and create a new folder named **HemletsLtd**.

◉   In the **File Name** box, type the name **Hemlets** (no spaces).

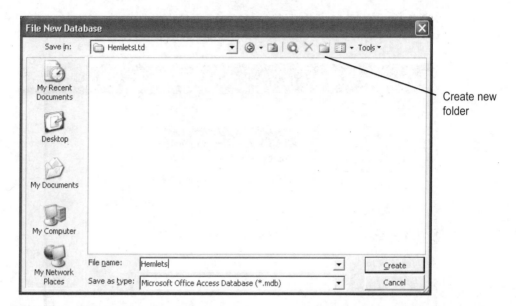

Create new folder

◉   Click the **Create** button. Access will automatically add the file extension **.mdb**.

Tip:
It is a good idea to keep each Access database in its own folder.

The database structure

The first thing you have to do is set up the database structure. As you learned in the last chapter, all data in an Access database is stored in tables. Each table has a row for each record and a column for each field. The first thing you have to do is tell Access exactly what fields you want in each record, and what data type each field is. After this has been done and the structure is saved, you can start adding data to the database.

The Database window

Access databases are made up of **objects**. A **table** is an object, and is the only object we have talked about so far. Other objects, which you will come across in this book, include **Queries**, **Forms** and **Reports**.

Every Access Database has a **Database window**. This is a sort of central menu for your database, from which you can open the objects in your database. The window has buttons (or tabs in Access 7 & 97) for each type of database object (Tables, Queries, Forms, Reports, etc.).

Tables is currently selected, and since at the moment there are no existing tables to **Open** or **Design**, only the **Create** options are active.

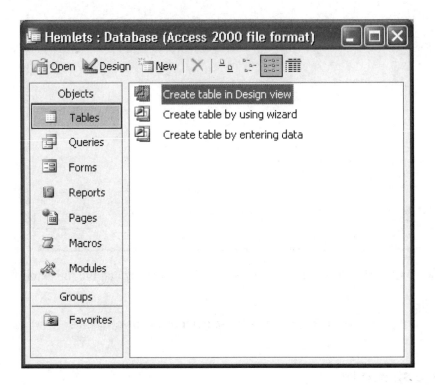

Hiding and displaying toolbars

You will learn about what individual toolbars and buttons do as they become relevant whilst you are creating your database. Here are a few tips that apply to all toolbars, which will be useful if you cannot find a particular toolbar or think that you are missing a button or two! You may find that you already know most of this – it will be pretty much the same as you have experienced in other Microsoft applications such as **Word** or **Excel**.

❶   You can select which toolbars are displayed on your screen. If you can't find a particular button it might be worth checking that you have the right toolbar displayed.

○ Select **View, Toolbars** and select the toolbar you want from the list that appears.

❶ This list will change according to what you are doing, as only a selection of toolbars will be relevant to what you are doing at any one time.

❶ You can hide a toolbar by selecting **View, Toolbars** and deselecting the toolbar.

Using the Help functions

If at any time you aren't sure how to do something in **Access**, you can search the **Help** files for instructions on your chosen subject. For example, let's search for help on **creating a table**.

○ Select **Help, Microsoft Office Access Help** from the menu.

You will see the **Office Assistant** appear.

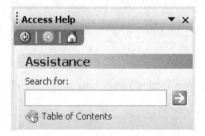

○ Type **create table** into the **Search for:** box, then click the **Start searching** button.

○ Select **About creating a table (MDB)** from the next pop-up box.

A Help window appears giving information on this topic. There's a lot of information here!

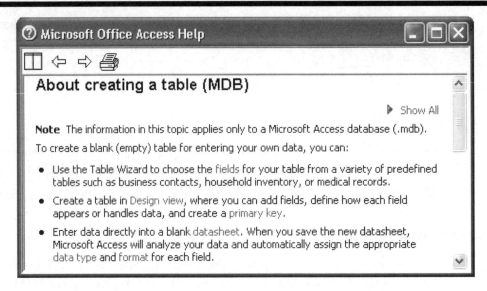

○ Click the red **Close** button when you have finished using **Help**.

Tip:
Next we'll create a table using the second method mentioned - **Create a table in Design view**.

Creating a new table

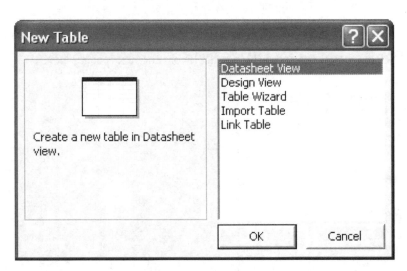

○ In the Database window make sure the **Tables** tab is selected, and click **New**.

A **New Table** window appears as shown below:

○ Select **Design View** and click **OK**.

The **Table Design** window appears.

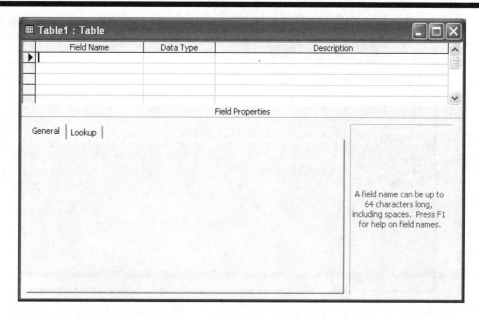

Look back at the structure of the **tblProperty** table on Page 5-11. All these fields need to be entered in the new table.

○ Enter the first field name, **PropertyRef**, and tab to the **Data Type** column. This will automatically enter **Text** as the data type, but we want **AutoNumber**, so click the small down-arrow to the right of the field and select **AutoNumber** from the list.

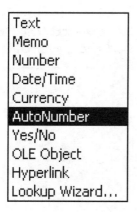

○ Tab to the **Description** column and type **This is the Key field**.

○ We'll leave the **Field Size** as **Long Integer**.

Defining the primary key

Every table in an Access database must have a primary key (also known as the key field). The field which you specify for the primary key must have a different value for each record. For the **Property** table we will set **PropertyRef** to be the primary key.

○ With the cursor in the row for the **PropertyRef**, click the **Primary Key** icon on the toolbar. The key symbol appears in the left-hand margin next to **PropertyRef**.

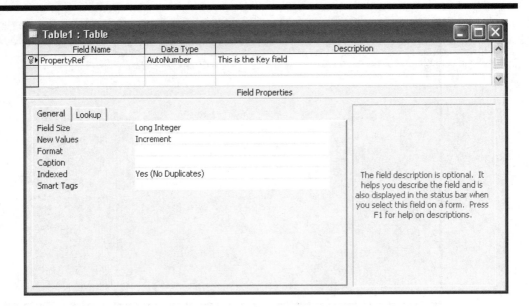

Entering other fields

Now we can enter all the other fields.

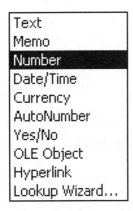   In the next row enter the field name as **Style** and leave the data type as **Text**. Enter the **Field Size** as **15**.

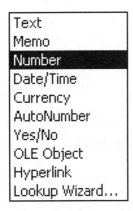   In the third row enter **Bedrooms** as the field name. Tab to the **Data Type** column and click the small down-arrow that appears. Select **Number** from the list of data types. Notice that in **Field Properties** the **Field Size** is automatically set to **Long Integer**.

```
Text
Memo
Number
Date/Time
Currency
AutoNumber
Yes/No
OLE Object
Hyperlink
Lookup Wizard...
```

Tip:
Note that **Field Properties** always appear at the bottom of the screen.

○ Enter the field name **Rent** and give it a data type **Currency**. Click below in the **Field Properties**. Notice that in **Field Properties** the **Decimal Places** is set to **Auto**. We don't want any decimal places, as the rent will always be in whole pounds. Click where it says **Auto** then click the small down-arrow on the right; click **0**.

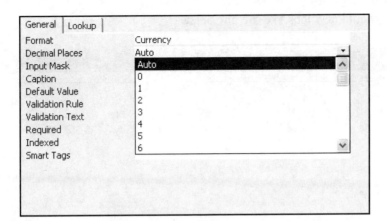

○ On the next row enter the field name **Rented** and give it a data type **Yes/No**. Click below in **Field Properties** – notice that there are different types of **Yes/No** fields available – you can also choose **True/False** or **On/Off**. We will leave it as **Yes/No**.

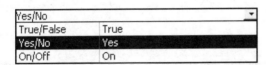

○ Next, enter the field name **LeaseExpiry** (one word) and give it a data type **Date/Time**. Again, there are several formats available to choose from in **Field Properties**. Click on the down-arrow next to the **Format** row and choose **Short Date** from the list.

Format		
Input Mask	General Date	19/06/1994 17:34:23
Caption	Long Date	19 June 1994
Default Value	Medium Date	19-Jun-94
Validation Rule	Short Date	19/06/1994
Validation Text	Long Time	17:34:23
Required	Medium Time	05:34 PM
Indexed	Short Time	17:34
IME Mode	No Control	
IME Sentence Mode	None	
Smart Tags		

○ Finally enter the field name **LandlordRef** with a data type **Text**. In **Field Properties**, set the **Field size** to **4**.

Tip:

Don't worry if you make a few mistakes - after all the fields are entered, you will learn how to move fields around, delete them or insert new fields. You can correct any mistakes at that point and it will be good practice.

Your table should now look like the one below:

Row selectors

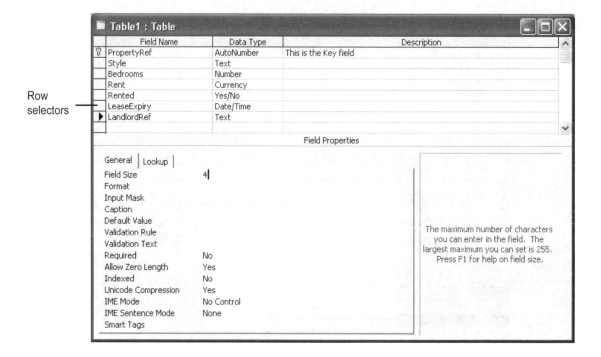

Saving the table structure

○ Save the table structure by clicking the **Save** icon or selecting **File**, **Save** from the menu bar. Don't worry if you've made some mistakes in the table structure – they can be corrected in a minute.

○ You will be asked to type a name for your table. Type the name **tblProperty** and click **OK**.

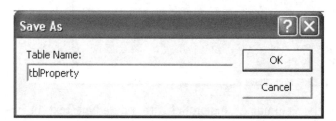

○ Click the **Close** icon in the top right-hand corner of the table to close the window. You will be returned to the Database window.

In the Database window you will see that your new table is now listed.

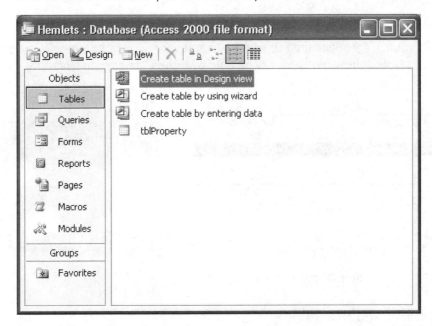

Tip:
If you have named the table wrongly, or made a spelling mistake, right-click the name in the main Database window and select **Rename**. Then type in the correct name. To delete a table, select it and press the **Delete** key on the keyboard.

Editing a table structure

   ○ Select the table name **tblProperty**, click the **Design View** icon and you are returned to **Design View**.

Inserting a field

To insert a new row for a **TotalRooms** column just above **Rent**:

○ Click the row selector (see the figure on Page 5-22) for **Rent**.

   ○ Press the **Insert** key on the keyboard or click the **Insert Rows** icon on the toolbar.

○ Enter the new field name **TotalRooms**, data type **Number**.

Deleting a field

Now, to delete the field you have just inserted:

○ Select the field by clicking in its row selector.

   ○ Press the **Delete** key on the keyboard or click the **Delete Rows** icon on the toolbar.

If you make a mistake, you can use **Edit, Undo Delete** from the top menu bar to restore the field.

Moving a field

◉ Click the row selector to the left of the field name to select the field.

◉ Click again and drag to where you want the field to be. You will see a line appear between fields as you drag over them to indicate where the field will be placed.

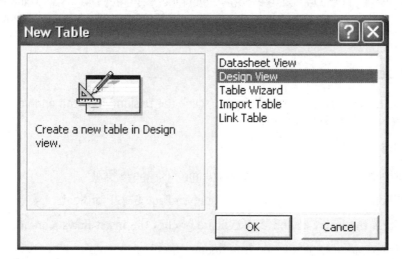

	Field Name	Data Type
🔑	PropertyRef	AutoNumber
	Style	Text
▶	Bedrooms	Number
	Rent	Currency
	Rented	Yes/No
	LeaseExpiry	Date/Time
	LandlordRef	Text

Tip:
The row selector is the square to the left of the field name

◉ Move the fields back so that your table looks like the one on Page 5-22 when you have finished experimenting.

◉ Close the **tblProperty** table.

Creating the tblLandlord table

We'll do this in just the same way as the **tblProperty** table.

[New] ───◉ From the Database window, make sure **Tables** is selected and click **New**.

New Table ? ✕

Create a new table in Design view.

- Datasheet View
- Design View
- Table Wizard
- Import Table
- Link Table

OK   Cancel

◉ Select **Design View** and click **OK**.

◉ Enter the first field name, **LandlordRef** and give it a data type **Text**. Later we will be linking the two tables using this field, and the **LandlordRef** field in the **tblProperty** table. It is very important that the two fields have the same data type and field properties or you won't be able to link the tables.

◉ Give **LandlordRef** a field length of **4** just as you did in the **tblProperty** table.

[🔑] ───◉ Make **LandlordRef** the key field by making sure the cursor is in the right row and clicking the **Primary Key** icon.

○ Enter the other field names, data types and field properties just as they were defined in the last chapter. Don't forget to enter the correct field lengths!

Your table should now look like the one below:

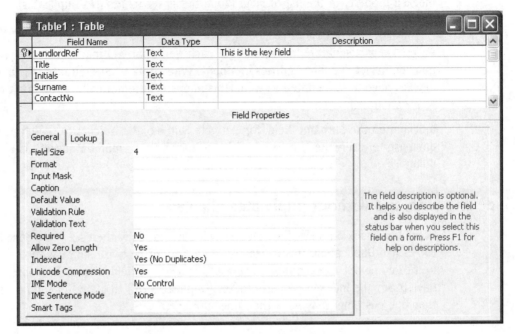

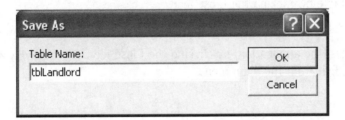

○ Save the table as **tblLandlord** by clicking the **Save** icon.

Editing field size attributes

If you have made any mistakes in field names or field sizes, you can edit them now. Remember, it is easy to make changes to the table structure BEFORE you enter any data. If you change field size attributes AFTER data has been entered, this may cause problems. For example:

❶ if you change the field size of the **LandlordRef** field in this table, it may no longer link correctly to another table.

❶ if you change the field size of **Surname** from 20 to 15, some surnames already in the database may be truncated if they are longer than 15 characters.

Indexing

When a field is defined as a primary key, it is automatically **indexed** by Access. For example in **tblLandlord**, if you click in the **LandlordRef** row, you will see that the **Indexed** property in the list of Field Properties is set to **Yes (No Duplicates)**.

Any other field can also be indexed simply by changing its **Indexed** property to **Yes**.

Access keeps a separate Index table for each field that you index, with the record number, rather like index entries in a book. When data is entered into the table, all the indexes have to be updated as well. (This happens automatically – you don't have to worry about it!)

Indexing on the **Surname** field, for example, will make it quicker to search a very large database for everyone with a particular surname. On a small database it is not worth doing.

Indexing with and without duplicates allowed

When you index on a key field, Access will automatically then set the **Indexed** property to **Yes (No Duplicates)**. This is because there cannot be two records with the same value in the key field. However, if you choose to index on a field such as **Surname**, you would have to set the **Indexed** property to **Yes (Duplicates OK)** to allow for the fact that more than one customer may have the same surname.

Closing the database application

- Close the table by clicking the **Close** icon.

- Close the database by clicking the **Close** icon in the Database window.

- Close Access (the application) by clicking the **Close** icon. Alternatively, you can select **File**, **Exit** from the main menu.

Exercise

This exercise is based on creating a new database table/file for an examining board. Part of the file creation is the appropriate design of the fields, including the type and size of fields.

1. Open your database application. Open a new blank database and save as **ExamBoard.mdb**.

2. Design a table with 3 fields using the appropriate data types and field sizes. The following fields must be created for the table: **CandidateID**, **Surname**, **Initials**.

3. Save the table as **Candidate**.

4. Save and close the database.

5. Close the database application.

Setting up Relationships

In the first chapter we looked at the relationships between the tables, and drew entity-relationship diagrams to represent the relationships. Now that the tables have been created we must link them in Access.

Relationships window

◉ On the main toolbar, click **Tools**, **Relationships**.

The **Show Table** window will appear:

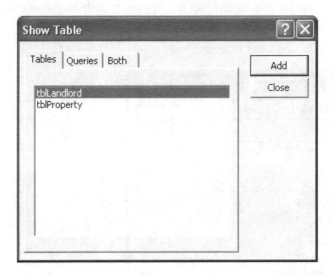

Tip:
If the Show Table window doesn't appear, just click the **Show Table** icon in the menu bar.

We want to form relationships between the two tables, so we want both tables to appear in the relationships window.

◉ Highlight each one in turn and click **Add**.

◉ Click **Close**.

The two tables will now appear in the relationships window as shown below.

◉ Click and drag the blue border at the bottom of the **tblProperty** table so that you can see all the field names.

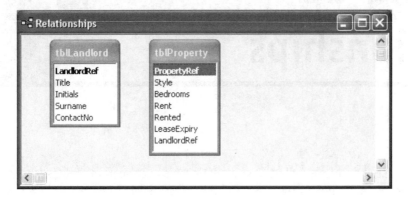

Creating a relationship

You will recall from the first chapter that we want a **one-to-many** relationship between **tblLandlord** and **tblProperty**.

◉ Click and drag the field **LandlordRef** from **tblLandlord** and drop it onto the field **LandlordRef** at the bottom of **tblProperty**. Always drag from the **one** side to the **many** side of the relationship.

The **Edit Relationships** window will appear:

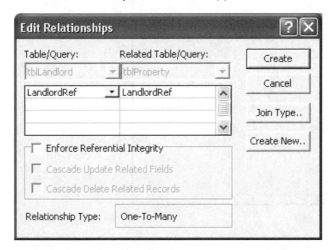

Notice that there are several options here. We'll go through what each of them means now. First here's a quick run through of which table is from which side of the relationship:

❶ **tblLandlord** is the table on the **one** side of the relationship.

❶ **tblProperty** is the table on the **many** side of the relationship.

❶ **LandlordRef** is the field which links the two tables.

Enforce Referential Integrity

You can enforce referential integrity if:

❶ the table on the **one** side of the relationship has a **Primary key**. In this example the table on the **one** side is the **tblLandlord** table, which does have a Primary key, **LandlordRef**.

❶ The link fields have the same data type and length. In this example the link field is **LandlordRef**; we have given this field the same data type **Text**, length **4**, in both tables.

If you enforce referential integrity, the following rules apply:

❶ You can't enter a value into the **many** side of the relationship that doesn't exist in the **one** side. In this example, you must enter the landlord's details into **tblLandlord** before you can enter the properties that the landlord owns into **tblProperty**.

❶ You can't delete a record from a table in the **one** side of a relationship if related records exist in the **many** table. This means that you can't delete a landlord's details in **tblLandlord** if there are properties in **tblProperty** that the landlord owns. If you want to be able to delete a landlord and automatically delete the properties that the landlord owns at the same time you would use **Cascade Delete**, which is explained below.

If you choose **Enforce Referential Integrity**, you are given the option of **Cascade Update Related Fields** and **Cascade Delete Related Fields**.

Cascade Update Related Fields

Cascade Update means that if you change the related field (in our case the related field is **LandlordRef**) in the **one** side of the relationship, Access will automatically update related fields in the **many** side. This means that if you change a Landlord's **LandlordRef** in tblLandlord, the **LandlordRef** will automatically be changed in all related records in tblProperty.

Cascade Delete Related Fields

Choosing **Cascade Delete** means that if you delete a record from a table on the **one** side of a relationship, all related records on the **many** side will automatically be deleted. For example, if you delete a landlord in **tblLandlord**, all properties that the landlord owns will automatically be deleted from **tblProperty**.

That's a lot of information! Don't worry too much if you can't take it all in at once. If you ever need a recap you can always just type **referential integrity** into the **Help Answer Wizard**.

Creating the relationship

> ● First we'll try creating the relationship without enforcing referential integrity, so just click **Create** without checking any of the boxes.

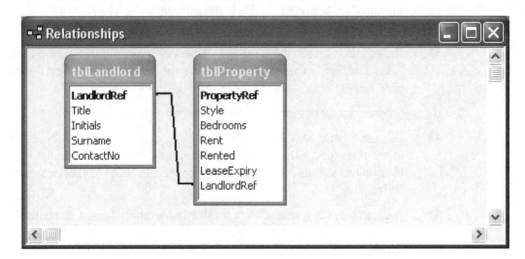

Notice that there is now a black line between the tables to represent the relationship. Because we didn't enforce referential integrity, Access has created a one-to-one relationship.

Deleting relationships

We want a one-to-many relationship with enforced referential integrity, so we will delete the relationship we just created then create a new one.

> ● Right-click the black line between the tables and select **Delete** from the shortcut menu.

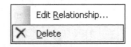

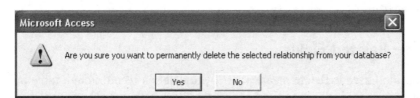

> ● Click **Yes** when asked to confirm the delete.

Now we'll create the new relationship.

> ● Click and drag the field **LandlordRef** from **tblLandlord** onto **LandlordRef** in **tblProperty**.

○ This time, click in the box to **Enforce Referential Integrity**.

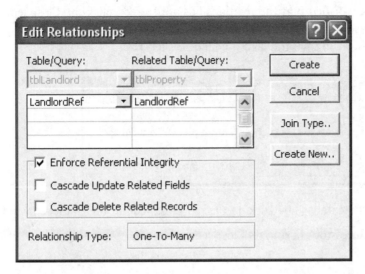

○ Click **Create**.

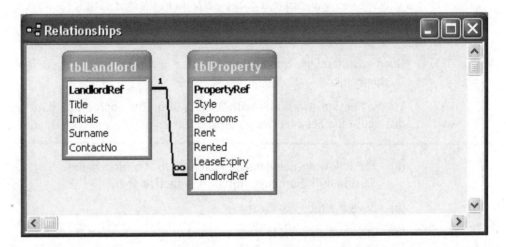

Notice that there is now a black line representing a **one-to-many** relationship between the two tables.

Word of warning!

When there is no data in the database it is very easy to edit the relationships. Once you have entered data, it will still be possible to edit the relationships but this is not advisable. If you change a relationship after data has been entered, Access may get confused, and you could find error messages appearing at inconvenient moments.

Saving the relationships

When you are satisfied that the relationships are correct, click the **Close** icon to return to the Database window. The relationships will automatically be saved, but you will be asked if you want to save the layout changes. Click **Yes**.

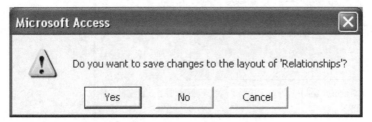

○   Close the database by clicking the red **Close** icon in the Database window.

○   Close Access by clicking its **Close** icon.

Exercise

In this exercise you will create a database and enter some data for a book shop. Part of the file creation is the appropriate design of the fields, including the type and size of fields.

1.   Open your database application. Create a new database and save it as **Customer.mbd**.

2.   You will design two tables with 4 fields using the appropriate data types, distinguishing between text, numeric, currency etc., and with appropriate field sizes.

    (a). The following fields must be created for the first table:
        CustomerID, Surname, Initials, ContactNumber.

    (b). Save the table as **Customer**.

    (c). The following fields must be created for the second table:
        OrderNumber, Date, Price, Description.

    (d). Save the table as **Orders**.

3.   Relate the tables using a one-to-many relationship. The **Customer** table should be on the one side and the **Orders** table on the many.

Datasheet View

Opening an existing database

○ Load Access. The following window will appear.

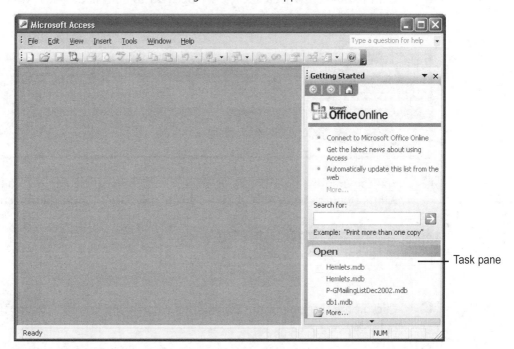

Task pane

○ Select **Hemlets.mdb** from the Task pane.

Tip:

If the right-hand pane does not appear, click File, Open from the menu bar and find the database. It should be in a folder named HemletsLtd.

The Database window will appear.

Table views

There are two **view modes** to choose from when making changes to your database:

- ❶ **Design View** is used for making changes to the database **structure**, for example adding a field or changing a field name. This is the view that you used in the last chapter to set up the database structure of the **Hemlets** database.

- ❶ **Datasheet View** is used for entering and editing the data held in the database. In this chapter we will be using **Datasheet View** to enter information about the properties and landlords into the **tblProperty** and **tblLandlord** tables.

Entering data

Because of the referential integrity rules, we will enter the data into the **one** side of the relationship first – i.e. the **tblLandlord** table.

 ⬤ With **tblLandlord** selected, click the **Open** button in the Database window.

The table now appears in **Datasheet view** as shown below:

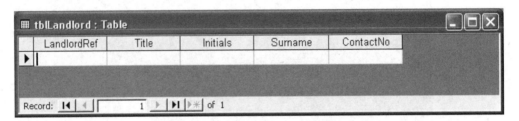

⬤ You can drag the right border of any column header (field name) to alter its width. Drag the borders so that the whole row easily fits on the screen.

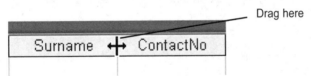

Drag here

⬤ Click in the first row of the **LandlordRef** column and enter **L1**. Tab to **Title** and enter **Mrs**.

⬤ Tab across and enter the initial as **J**. Go to the **Surname** field and enter **Welsh**. Enter **01474 276499** as the **ContactNo**.

Your table should now look like the one below:

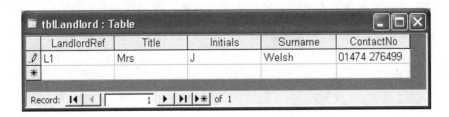

◐ Now enter the rest of the data as shown in the following table.

LandlordRef	Title	Initials	Surname	ContactNo
L1	Mrs	J	Welsh	01474 276499
L2	Mr	S	Hemmings	01474 572772
L3	Mr	M	Jenkins	01474 387465
L4	Mr	M	Stevenson	01474 783748
L5	Miss	L	Vacher	01474 583689
L6	Mrs	J	Hemmings	01474 856683

◐ When you have entered all the data, click the **Close** icon in the top right-hand corner of the current window. (Be careful to close just the table window, not Access.)

◐ If you have changed the column widths, you will be asked if you want to save the changes you made to the layout.

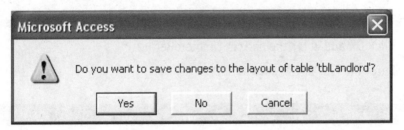

◐ Click **Yes**. You will be returned to the Database window.

Entering data for tblProperty

◐ From the Database window, make sure **tblProperty** is selected and click **Open**.

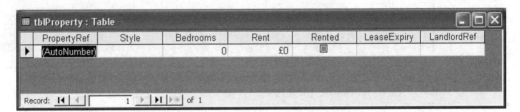

◐ Click in the first row of the **PropertyRef** column, where it says **(AutoNumber)**. Access will automatically put a value in here, so you don't have to enter anything.

◐ Tab to **Style** and enter **Semi**. Enter **3** as the number of bedrooms.

◐ Tab to the **Rent** column and enter **800**; don't worry if the pound sign has been deleted – it will reappear when you leave the field.

◑   Click in the checkbox in the **Rented** column to indicate a **Yes**.

Tip:
Pressing the **Space** bar in the **Rented** field will have the same effect as ticking the checkbox.

◑   In the **Lease Expiry** column, enter **1/6/03**. Notice that when you tab out of the field Access changes it to **01/06/2003**.

◑   Try entering **L9** as the **LandlordRef**, and pressing the **Enter** key. You should get the following error message:

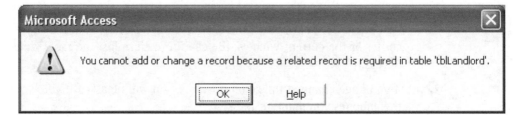

Microsoft Access

You cannot add or change a record because a related record is required in table 'tblLandlord'.

OK   Help

This is because there is no landlord with **LandlordRef** L9 entered in **tblLandlord**.

◑   Click **OK** and enter the correct **LandlordRef**, **L1**.

◑   Enter the rest of the data as shown below:

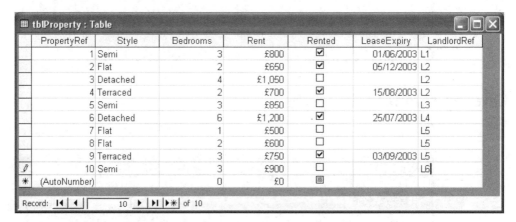

tblProperty : Table

PropertyRef	Style	Bedrooms	Rent	Rented	LeaseExpiry	LandlordRef
1	Semi	3	£800	☑	01/06/2003	L1
2	Flat	2	£650	☑	05/12/2003	L2
3	Detached	4	£1,050	☐		L2
4	Terraced	2	£700	☑	15/08/2003	L2
5	Semi	3	£850	☐		L3
6	Detached	6	£1,200	☑	25/07/2003	L4
7	Flat	1	£500	☐		L5
8	Flat	2	£600	☐		L5
9	Terraced	3	£750	☑	03/09/2003	L5
10	Semi	3	£900	☐		L6
(AutoNumber)		0	£0	▨		

Record: ◄◄ ◄ [10] ► ►► ►✳ of 10

◑   Save and close the table.

Viewing data in a table

○ In the Database window, make sure that **Tables** is selected in the list of objects on the left of the window.

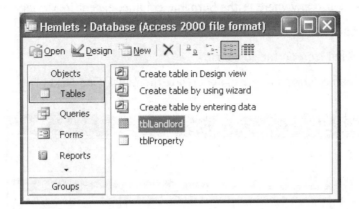

○ Select **tblLandlord** and click **Open**. This will open the table in **Datasheet View**. (If you wanted to change the actual structure of the table, for example to add a new field, you would select **Design**.)

The table appears as shown below:

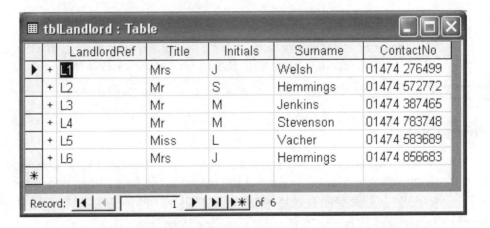

Using the record selectors

You can navigate to the next or previous record using the record selectors in **Datasheet View**. You can also move to the first or last record, or to a new record at the end of the database.

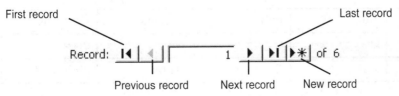

Finding a record

Sometimes you may want to search for the record for a particular landlord. Again, this is most useful on a much larger database.

O   Click the mouse anywhere in the **Surname** column, except in Mr. Jenkins' record.

Suppose you want to find the record for **Mr Jenkins**.

O   Click the **Find** icon on the toolbar.

O   Type the name **Jenkins** in the dialogue box then click **Find Next**.

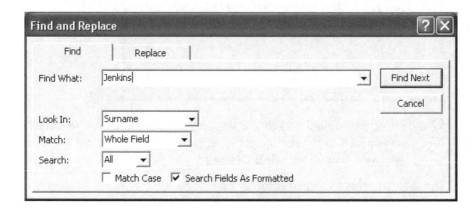

Mr Jenkins' record should now be highlighted.

O   You can use **wildcards** such as * in a search. Try searching for **H***. This will find the next record starting with **H** each time you click **Find Next**.

O   Close the **Find and Replace** window by clicking its **Close** icon.

Modifying data

You can change the contents of any field (except **PropertyRef** which, being an **Autonumber** field, is set by Access) by clicking in the field and editing in the normal way. Use the **Backspace** or **Delete** key to delete unwanted text and type the corrections.

Remember you can undo changes using the **Undo** icon.

Adding a new record

Suppose two new landlords have registered with **Hemlets**, and their details have to be added to the **Hemlets** database. Their details are shown below:

LandlordRef	Title	Initials	Surname	ContactNo
L7	Mr	I	Iqbal	01474 733543
L8	Miss	E	Harrison	01474 898398

There are two ways to add a new record:

- *Either* click in the next blank line,
- *or* click the **New Record** icon on either the record selector (see the figure on the previous page) or the **Table Datasheet** toolbar.
- Enter **Mr Iqbal's** and **Miss Harrison's** details from the table above.

The first method is easy for such a small database, but if there were hundreds of landlords in the database you wouldn't want to scroll down to an empty row. For larger databases you would use the **New Record** icon.

Deleting a record

To delete Mr Iqbal's record:

- Click anywhere in Mr Iqbal's record.
- Click the **Delete** icon on the toolbar. You will see a message:

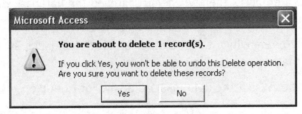

- Click **Yes** to delete the record.
- Save and close the table, then close the database.

Exercise

1. (a) Open the database **ExamBoard.mdb** created in Chapter 2.

   (b) Add the following records:

CandidateID	Surname	Initials
1	Benaud	RJ
2	Matthews	SE
3	King	AE
4	Thompson	G
5	Adams	QH
6	Matthews	D

2. (a) Open the database **Customer.mdb** that you created in the last chapter.

   (b) Enter 4 new customer records.

   (c) For each of these customers, enter 2 orders in the Orders table.

   (d) Save and close this database.

Data Validation

Access can help to make sure that you have entered the data correctly into the database. If you make a mistake entering data, especially in very large databases, the error can be very difficult to trace. For example, if you entered **Terrace** instead of **Terraced** as the style for a property, then when you searched the database for properties where the style was entered as **Terraced**, that record wouldn't be shown.

Although there are many errors which the database cannot detect (such as a misspelt name), there are many that it can.

You can write a set of rules which the data must abide by. For example:

❶ The style of a property can only be **Flat**, **Terraced**, **Semi** or **Detached**.

❶ The number of bedrooms must be between **1** and **9**.

❶ The rent must be between **200** and **5000**.

❶ The lease expiry date must be entered as a date later than today's date. The validation rule will only be applied when the date is entered – it doesn't matter if the date becomes invalid some months after it is has been entered.

The process of checking that the data meets various 'rules' is called **validation**. The rules themselves are called **validation rules**.

Alongside each rule, you can enter some text that Access will show to the user if they enter invalid data. This is called **validation text**.

Comparison operators

There are several **comparison operators** that you can use, and they are listed in the table below:

Operator	Meaning	Example
<	less than	<20
<=	less than or equal to	<=20
>	greater than	>0
>=	greater than or equal to	>=0
=	equal to	=20 ="Flat" OR "Terraced"
<>	not equal to	<>"Semi"
BETWEEN	test for a range of values. Must be two comparison values (a low & high value) separated by AND operator	BETWEEN 01/12/2002 AND 25/12/2002

Entering the validation rules

○ Open the **Hemlets** database.

○ In the Database window, make sure the **Tables** tab is selected then click to select **tblProperty**.

 ○ Click **Design** to open the table in **Design View**.

We are going to enter a validation rule for the **Style** field. The rule we will use is: **Style** can only be **Flat, Terraced, Semi** or **Detached**.

○ Click in the **Style** field name.

Notice that two of the rows in the **Field Properties** at the bottom of the screen are named **Validation Rule** and **Validation Text**. This is where we will enter the rules.

○ In the **Field Properties** click in the **Validation Rule** row.

○ Type **Flat or Terraced or Semi or Detached** and press **Enter**. Notice when you tab out of this field that Access will add quotes.

○ In the **Validation Text** row type **The style must be Flat, Terraced, Semi or Detached**.

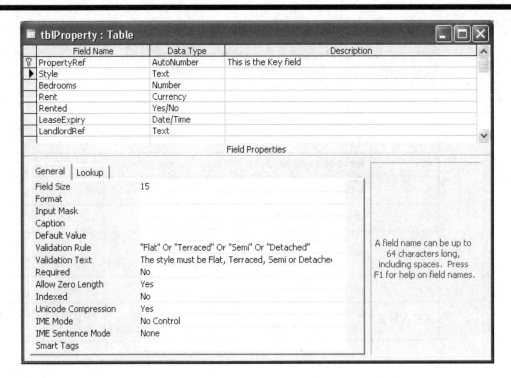

● Return to **Datasheet View** by clicking the **Datasheet View** icon.

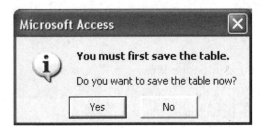

● You will be asked to save the changes you have just made. Click **Yes**, and **Yes** again to the prompt about data integrity rules.

Testing the validation rule

We will test the rule by entering a new record that does not agree with the validation rule.

Property Ref	Style	Bedrooms	Rent	Rented	Lease Expiry	Landlord Ref
(Auto Number)	Semi detached	3	775	N		L3

● Click in the empty row below the last property. The **PropertyRef** will be entered automatically, so tab to the **Style** field and type **Semi detached**. Press **Enter**.

A message will appear on the screen containing the Validation Text that you entered:

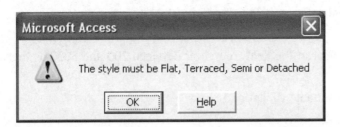

- Click **OK**. Re-enter the style as **Semi** and press **Enter**. Access should accept this.
- Enter the rest of the details for this property from the table above.

Tip:

Access will not allow you to exit the field until the value in that field meets the validation rule.

Setting the other validation rules

Now we'll set a validation rule for the **Bedrooms** field. The rule we'll use is: The number of bedrooms must be between **1** and **9**.

- Return to **Design View** by clicking the **Design View** icon.
- Click in the **Bedrooms** field.
- Enter the **Validation Rule** and **Validation Text** as shown below:

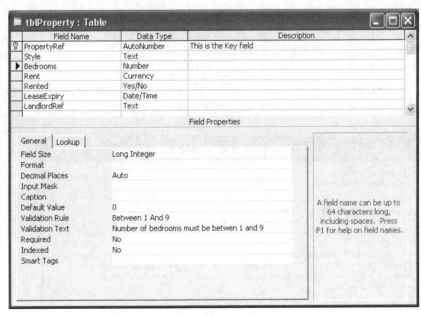

You can press F1 for help if you get stuck!

Entering a validation rule for Rent

You can enter a validation rule for a **Currency** field in just the same way as a **Number** field.

◉ With the cursor in the **Rent** row, enter **Between 200 and 5000** as the validation rule.

◉ Enter some suitable validation text.

Entering a validation rule for a Date field

This is also quite straightforward. We want to enter the following rule: the **Lease Expiry** must be between **1/1/2003** and **1/1/2008**.

◉ Make sure the cursor is in the **Lease Expiry** row of the **tblProperty** table.

◉ Enter the rule **between #1/1/03# and #1/1/08# or null** as the validation rule. Enter some suitable validation text.

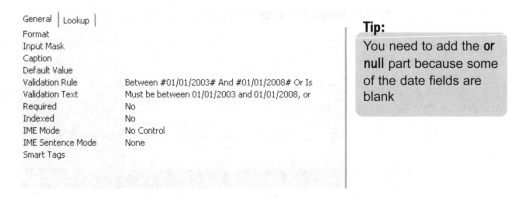

General	Lookup
Format	
Input Mask	
Caption	
Default Value	
Validation Rule	Between #01/01/2003# And #01/01/2008# Or Is
Validation Text	Must be between 01/01/2003 and 01/01/2008, or
Required	No
Indexed	No
IME Mode	No Control
IME Sentence Mode	None
Smart Tags	

Tip:
You need to add the **or null** part because some of the date fields are blank

❶ When using a date in a validation rule, you must put it between **#** marks, so an ordinary date **1/1/03** becomes **#1/1/03#**. You don't need to remember all this – if you get stuck, just look up **validation rule** in the **Help Answer Wizard**, or press **F1** when your cursor is in the **Validation Rule** row.

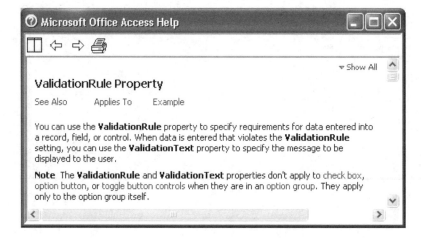

⑦ **Microsoft Office Access Help** ▢ ▢ ✕

▽ Show All

ValidationRule Property

See Also   Applies To   Example

You can use the **ValidationRule** property to specify requirements for data entered into a record, field, or control. When data is entered that violates the **ValidationRule** setting, you can use the **ValidationText** property to specify the message to be displayed to the user.

Note The **ValidationRule** and **ValidationText** properties don't apply to check box, option button, or toggle button controls when they are in an option group. They apply only to the option group itself.

More testing!

- Return to **Datasheet View** by clicking the **Datasheet View** icon.

- Click **Yes** to save the changes and **Yes** to the prompt about data integrity rules.

In the table below are more records that have to be entered.

- Try entering invalid values for **Bedrooms**, **Rent** and **Date**. You should see your error messages appearing!

Tip:
Always test your validation rules by trying to enter invalid data. You can press **Esc** to cancel the record without saving it.

PropertyRef	Style	Bed rooms	Rent	Rented	LeaseExpiry	LandlordRef
(Auto Number)	Detached	4	950	Y	19/8/03	L8
(Auto Number)	Semi	2	750	N		L4
(Auto Number)	Terraced	2	700	Y	5/1/04	L5

- When you have entered the records with the data shown, save and close your table.

- Close Access if this is the end of a session.

Exercise

In this exercise you will validate fields.

1. Open your database application Customer.mbd.

2. In the Orders table, set a validation rule so that the date entered cannot be earlier than 2003.

3. Set another rule so that the price cannot exceed £5,000.00 and warns the user with a suitable message if this happens.

4. Enter an order record and try out invalid values.

5. Save and close the database.

Sorting, Formatting and Printing

○ Open Access. Open the **Hemlets** database.

○ Double-click **tblProperty** to open it.

○ Reduce the size of this window and drag it to one side so that you can see the database window.

○ Double-click **tblLandlord** to open this table also.

Sorting records

Alphabetical sorts

You can perform a simple sort on one field by clicking anywhere in the column you want to sort on and clicking one of the two **Sort** buttons (**Sort Ascending** and **Sort Descending**) on the toolbar.

To sort the properties in the **tblLandlord** table by surname:

○ Click in the **Surname** field and click the **Sort Ascending** icon. The records will now be sorted in ascending order of surname, as shown below:

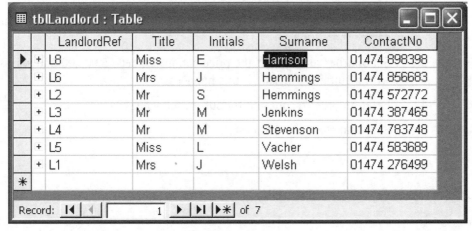

	LandlordRef	Title	Initials	Surname	ContactNo
▶ +	L8	Miss	E	Harrison	01474 898398
+	L6	Mrs	J	Hemmings	01474 856683
+	L2	Mr	S	Hemmings	01474 572772
+	L3	Mr	M	Jenkins	01474 387465
+	L4	Mr	M	Stevenson	01474 783748
+	L5	Miss	L	Vacher	01474 583689
+	L1	Mrs	J	Welsh	01474 276499
*					

Record: ◀◀ ◀ 1 ▶ ▶◀ ▶* of 7

○ Now click the **Sort Descending** button.

The records will be resorted in descending alphabetical order.

Numerical sorts

◐ Now click in the **Bedrooms** column of **tblProperties**.

◐ Click the **Sort Descending** button.

The records will be sorted in descending order of the number of bedrooms. You can try resorting them in ascending order of **Rent** now!

◐ When you have finished experimenting, close **tblProperties**.

Formatting and printing a datasheet

You can print a datasheet just as it is, or you can format it first by hiding unwanted columns, changing the order of the columns and changing column widths. We will practise these techniques.

◐ With **tblLandlord** open in **Datasheet View**, click the **Print Preview** icon. Your data appears as shown below:

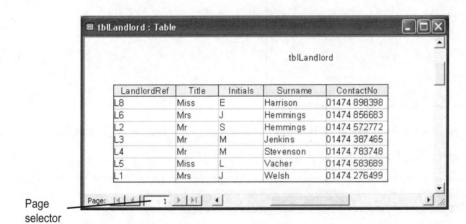

Page selector

Tip:
If it's too small to read, click on it to enlarge it.

A large datasheet may not fit on one page in **Portrait** view. You would use the page selector at the bottom of the screen to view the other pages.

The **Print Preview** toolbar appears at the top of the screen. You can **Zoom** in on a page by clicking anywhere on it, or by clicking the **Zoom** icon.

View one page   View two pages

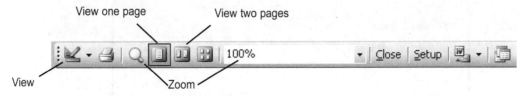

View   Zoom

◐ Click **Close** to exit **Print Preview**.

Changing the Page layout

You can change the page layout to **Landscape** view.

- ◗ Select **File**, **Page Setup** from the menu.
- ◗ Click the **Page** tab in the **Page Setup** dialogue box. Click **Landscape**.
- ◗ Click **OK**.

- ◗ Try another **Print Preview**. If it didn't fit on one page before, it should now.
- ◗ Select **File**, **Print** to print the datasheet.

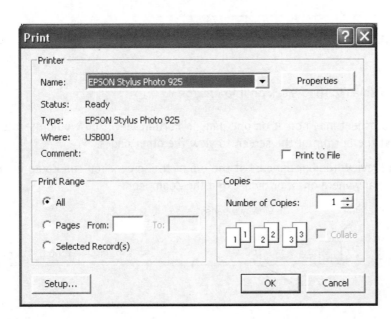

- ◗ Here you can decide which pages to print and how many copies to print. Click **OK** to print, otherwise click **Cancel**.

Printing only selected records

◐ With the table in **Datasheet View**, select just a few records by clicking and dragging across their row selectors.

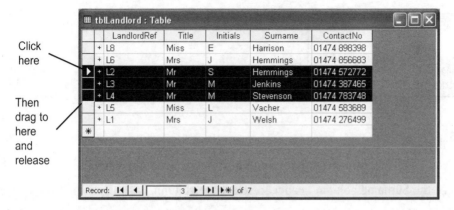

Click here

Then drag to here and release

◐ Select **File**, **Print** from the menu.

◐ Check the option **Selected Records** under the **Print Range** section.

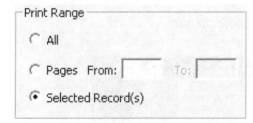

◐ Click **OK** to print only those records you highlighted.

Hiding and unhiding columns

Sometimes you may not want to print all the columns in the datasheet. You can hide the columns that you don't want.

◐ Make sure you have **tblLandlord** open in **Datasheet View**.

◐ Click on the column header for **LandlordRef**.

This is the LandlordRef column header

LandlordRef	Title	Initials	Surname	ContactNo
L8	Miss	E	Harrison	01474 898398
L6	Mrs	J	Hemmings	01474 856683
L2	Mr	S	Hemmings	01474 572772
L3	Mr	M	Jenkins	01474 387465
L4	Mr	M	Stevenson	01474 783748
L5	Miss	L	Vacher	01474 583689
L1	Mrs	J	Welsh	01474 276499

- From the menu select **Format, Hide Columns**. The column will be hidden.

- To unhide the column, just select **Format, Unhide Columns** from the menu, and tick the field you want to unhide.

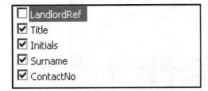

Moving columns

Suppose you want the **Surname** column to appear before the **Title** column.

- Click the **Surname** column header to select the column.

- Click again and hold down the mouse button, then drag the header to the left of the **Title** column. The table should now appear as shown below.

- Adjust the column widths by double-clicking in the column header on the border between each column.

Your table should now appear as shown below:

- Click the **Print Preview** icon again to see what the page will look like when printed out.

- Click the **Close** icon and click **Yes** when asked if you want to save changes to the table layout.

Exercise

1. Open the ExamBoard.mbd database.

2. Print the first four records of the Candidate table with fields in the order CandidateID, Surname, Initials.

3. Print all the records with fields in the order Surname, Initials, CandidateID.

4. Close the database.

Forms

User interface

You need to consider how the users interact with your computer application – how they choose what to do next, how they enter data and so on.

We will start by creating a form to allow the user to input data about landlords.

This form will be used to enter new landlords when they register with **Hemlets**.

Creating a new form

○ Make sure the **Hemlets** database is open.

 ○ In the Database window select the **Forms** tab.

One of the options is to use a **wizard**. This is usually the quickest method, and the one you normally use to create a simple form.

○ Click **New**. Click to select **Form Wizard**, and select **tblLandlord** from the dropdown list at the bottom of the **New Form** window.

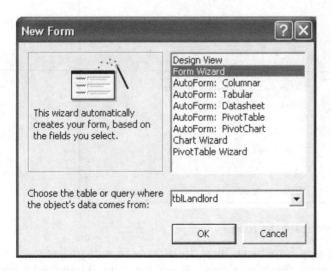

○ Click **OK**.

◗ You are now asked which fields you want to appear on your form. We want all the fields, so click >>. All the fields should now appear in the right-hand pane.

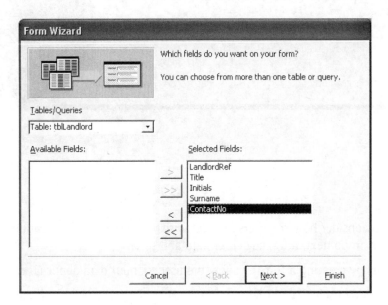

◗ Click **Next**. Leave the form layout as **Columnar** and click **Next**.

◗ Leave the style as **Standard**, click **Next**.

◗ Enter **frmLandlord** as the title of the form. We will change this title later, but we need to enter **frmLandlord** here so that Access will save the form with that name.

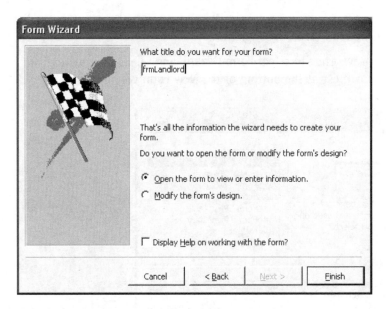

◗ Click **Finish** to create the form.

◗ The form opens in **Form View**. There are already records showing in the form – these are all the records you entered directly into the **tblLandlord** table.

Tip:
If the lengths of your fields look different to this it's probably because you didn't enter the correct **Field Size** for each field. You can change the **Field Size** property by opening **tblLandlord** in **Design View**; use the field sizes in the table on Page 5-12. The field sizes on the form will need to be adjusted manually now though.

Changing View mode

As with tables, you need to have the form open in **Design View** in order to modify it.

 Click the **Design View** icon to view the form in **Design View**.

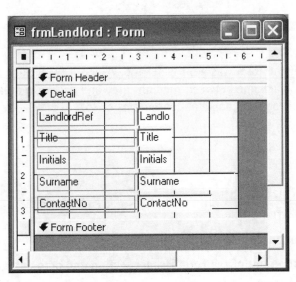

Adding text to the header

It would be nice to have a title for the form. On the form in **Design View**, notice there's a section at the top named **Form Header**. That's where we'll put the title.

First we need to expand the **Form Header** section because it currently has no space under it!

○ Place the cursor on the border between the **Form Header** and **Detail** section headers. The cursor should change to a double-headed arrow, like in the next screenshot.

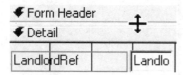

○ Click and drag the border downwards a couple of centimetres or so, as shown below:

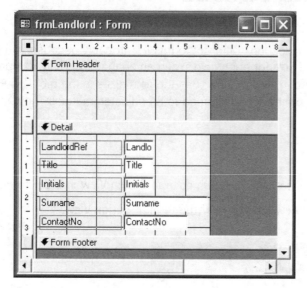

○ It would be nice if the form was a bit wider too. Widen it by clicking and dragging the thin black line between the light grey and dark grey areas of the form (see below). Drag it a couple of centimetres or so.

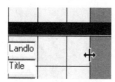

Now we've got space to write a title.

Aa ── ○ Click the **Label** icon in the **Toolbox**.

○ Now click in the top right of the **Form Header** section and drag out a rectangle as shown below:

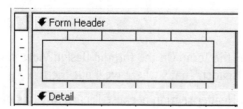

○ The text cursor will be flashing in the box, so you can now type the title. Type **Landlord Details Form**.

The text will appear quite small and uninteresting so we need to change the size and colour of the font.

○ Select the whole label box by first clicking away from the label then clicking once on it. When it is selected it should have handles around it.

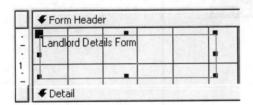

Now you can change the font size just as you would in **Word** or **Excel** – using the buttons on the **Formatting** toolbar.

The Formatting toolbar

Fill / Back Colour

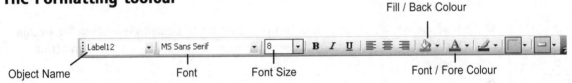

Object Name   Font   Font Size   Font / Fore Colour

○ If you cannot see the **Formatting** toolbar, go to **View, Toolbars,** then click the box next to **Formatting (Form/Report)**.

Changing text size

○ With the label selected, click the small down-arrow in the text size box. Click to select **14**.

Changing text colour

○ Click the small down-arrow on the **Font/Fore Color** button.

○ Just click to select a colour you like!

○ Try changing the background colour too, using the **Fill/Back Color** button.

○ Click and drag the handles so that the label box fills the whole **Form Header**.

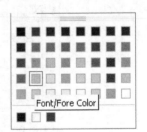
Font/Fore Color

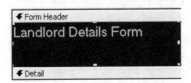

Now you can view how it will look by changing to **Form View**.

  ➲ Click the **Form View** icon to return to **Form View**.

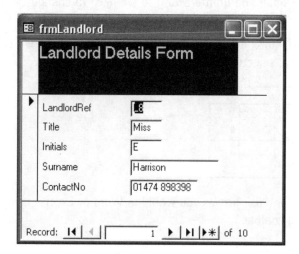

That looks pretty smart!

❸ If you're not happy with your form, just return to **Design View** using the **Design View** icon and play around some more with the functions on the **Formatting** toolbar.

  ➲ Whilst the data you enter into forms is automatically saved, you have to remember to save any changes you make to the design. Save your changes by clicking the **Save** icon, or by selecting **File**, **Save** from the menu.

Adding text to the footer

This is done in exactly the same way as the header, except we will use the **Form Footer** section instead of the **Form Header**.

➲ Return to **Design View**.

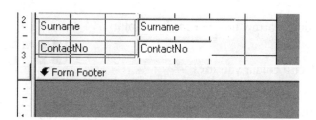

At the bottom of the form is the **Form Footer** section. It doesn't look like there is any room to write anything but the form will expand as soon as you put a label in the dark grey space below the **Form Footer** section header.

  ➲ Click the **Label** icon in the **Formatting** toolbar.

➲ Drag out a rectangle just like you did for the **Form Header**.

○ Type the text **Hemlets Database**.

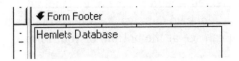

○ Change the font size and colour, and the background colour until you are happy with the way it looks. You can also change the size of the label box.

○ Go to **Form View** to see your handiwork!

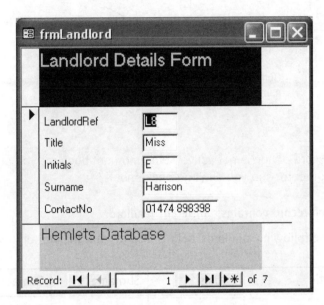

○ Try resizing the form by clicking and dragging the blue border round the form. You'll see that whatever size you make the form, the footer will remain at the bottom of the window.

Closing and opening a form

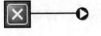 ○ Click the **Close** button to close the form. If you have made changes to the design of the form since you last saved, you will be asked if you want to save the changes. Click **Yes**.

In the Database window, you will see the name of the form, **frmLandlord**, appear whenever the **Forms** tab is selected. If you wanted to delete the form for any reason, you could do so by clicking the form name and pressing the **Delete** key. Not now!

○ Open the form again by double-clicking the form name.

Entering data using the form

Now we'll use the form you've just created to enter some more landlord details into the form. When using the form to enter or look up data, you will need to use the **Record Selectors**. These are the buttons you can see at the bottom of your form.

The Record selectors

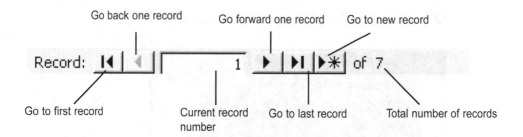

Tip:
The **Go back one record** button is not active at the moment because you are already on the first record – so you can't go back one.

❶   Remember each **record** contains a different **landlord**.

We will now enter the following landlords' details into the **tblLandlord** form.

LandlordRef	Title	Initials	Surname	ContactNo
L9	Mr	T	Hodson	01474 243046
L10	Mr	P	Chisholm	01474 384446
L11	Miss	F	Kennedy	01474 558374

◉   Go to a new record using the **New record** button on the record selectors.

◉   The cursor should now be in the **LandlordRef** box on the new record, so type **L9**.

◉   Either click in the **Title** box or just press tab. Enter **Mr**.

◉   Enter the remaining details for **Mr Hodson** using the table above.

Your form should now look like this:

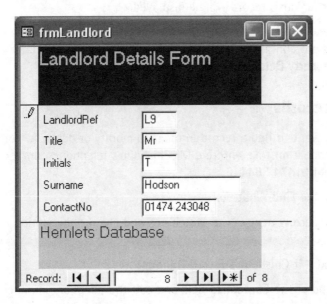

◗ Enter the other two landlords from the table on the previous page.

Going to specific records

You can use the record selectors to find records in a form.

◗ Flick through the records in the form using the **forward one** and **back one** record selectors.

❶ You can look up a specific record in the same way as you did in the table – using the **Find** button on the **Form View** toolbar. Alternatively, you can select **Find** from the **Edit** menu.

◗ With the cursor in the **Surname** field, click the **Find** button.

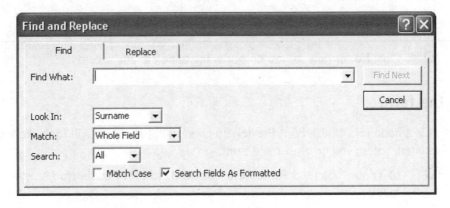

◗ Suppose you wanted to find the record for **Jenkins**. Type **Jenkins** into the **Find What** box.

○ Click **Find Next**. It may appear as if nothing has happened, but if you now look at your form, Mr Jenkins's record will be displayed.

Note that you can search for a record with a particular number or date in a field too. Since this form does not contain any dates or numbers we will try this later in the chapter using the **Property Details** form!

Using a form to modify records

Sometimes you may want to find a record in order to modify or delete it. For example, suppose you have made a mistake entering Mr Chisholm's telephone number – it should be 01474 384464, not 01474 384446.

○ Type **Chis** into the **Find What** box.

○ Click the down-arrow next to the Match box and change this option to **Any Part of Field**.

○ Click **Find Next**. Mr Chisholm's record will appear.

○ Click at the end of the **ContactNo** field and edit the telephone number.

Using a form to delete records

 You can delete the current record by clicking the **Delete Record** button when the record is displayed on the screen. You will see a message on the screen:

⚠ Microsoft Access
You are about to delete 1 record(s).

If you click Yes, you won't be able to undo this Delete operation.
Are you sure you want to delete these records?

[Yes]   [No]

○ Click **No** for now as you do not want to delete any records.

Printing the form

It is a good idea to use **Print Preview** to check what the form will look like when it is printed, before you go ahead and print.

 ○ Make sure you're in **Form View**. Click the **Print Preview** button on the **Form View** toolbar.

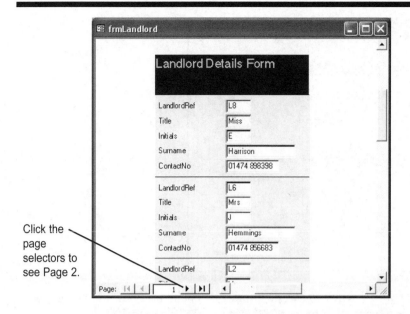

Click the page selectors to see Page 2.

Tip:
If the form is too small to read, just click it to enlarge it

○ Click **Close** to exit **Print Preview**.

Page setup

Use **Page Setup** to change the orientation of the paper and the paper size.

○ Select **File**, **Page Setup** from the menu.

○ Click the **Page** tab then click to select the orientation and paper size you want. Click **OK**.

○ To print, select **File**, **Print** from the menu.

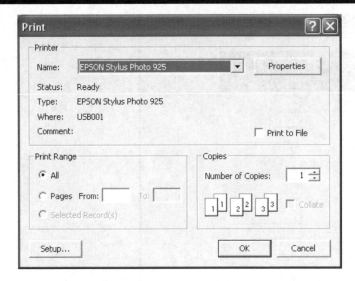

- ○ You can enter which pages you want to print here, and also how many copies you want. If you want to print, click **OK**, otherwise click **Cancel**.

- ○ Close your form by clicking the **Close** icon.

- ○ You may be asked if you want to save changes to the design. Click **Yes**.

The Property form

It would be nice to have a form to enter all the property details. Using exactly the same method you used for the **frmLandlord** form, try and create a form for the properties. Save it as **frmProperty**.

When you're done, it should look something like this:

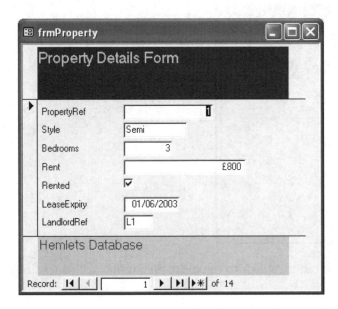

Try using the **Find** button to find all the two-bedroom properties. You can click the **Find Next** button in the **Find and Replace** window to scroll through them all.

You can also click in the **LeaseExpiry** field and find a record with a particular lease expiry date. Try finding the record with a lease expiry date of 05/12/2003.

Sorting data in forms

You can sort data in forms into ascending or descending numeric or alphabetical sequence. You have already practised sorting records in a table (see Chapter 5.6) and the procedure is exactly the same.

 Click in the field for **Rent** and click **the Sort Descending** button. This will sort the records in descending order of Rent. Scroll through the forms to satisfy yourself that this is so.

 Sort the records back to the original sequence by clicking in the **PropertyRef** field and clicking the **Sort Ascending** button.

That's all you need to know about forms, so now you can close your database and have a break!

 Close your database by clicking the close icon on the Database window. Close Access by clicking its **Close** icon.

Exercises

1. (a) Open the **ExamBoard.mdb** database.
   (b) Create a simple form to input data into your **Candidate** table.
   (c) Save the form as **frmCandidate**.
   (d) Enter 2 new records using the form.
   (e) Close the database.

2. (a) Open the **Customer.mdb** database.
   (b) Create a simple form to input data into your **Customer** table.

   Make all the text labels font size 14. Include a heading in a larger font on a shaded background. In the Footer section, insert the text **BetterBooks Ltd**.
   (c) Save the form as **frmCustomer**.
   (d) Enter 2 new records using the form.
   (e) Close the database.

Both filters and queries are used to select specific records (referred to as a **subset** of records) from a table of data.

❶   In general, you would use a filter to temporarily view or edit a subset of records while you're in a table or form. Queries are slightly more complicated but also perform useful tasks that cannot be done with a filter. You'll understand more about which is most appropriate once you've had a go at them.

Using a filter in a form

We'll use a filter to select specific types of records in the **frmLandlord** form.

▶   Open the **Hemlets** database, then open the **frmLandlord** form in **Form View**.

Notice the filter options on the **Form View** toolbar.

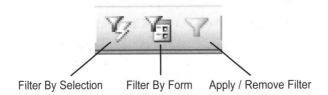

Filter By Selection   Filter By Form   Apply / Remove Filter

Filter by selection

With **filter by selection**, all you need to do is find one instance of the value you are looking for in the form.

We'll use **filter by selection** to select only those records where the title is **Miss**.

▶   Use the record selectors to navigate to any record where the title is **Miss**. Click in the **Title** field so that the cursor is in the same field as the **Miss** entry.

 ▶   Click the **Filter By Selection** button.

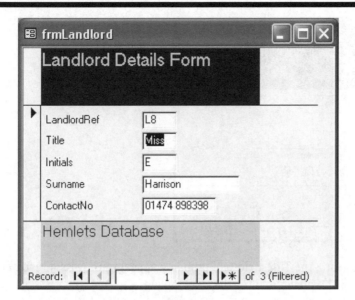

Look at the bottom of the form where the record selectors are – there are now only **3** records available to view.

○ Use the record selectors to scroll through the three selected records. They should all have the title **Miss**.

Removing the filter

——○ Remove the filter by clicking the **Remove Filter** button (this button changes name from **Apply Filter** to **Remove Filter** depending on whether you currently have a filter applied).

The form should return to normal with all **10** records available.

❸ You can toggle the filter on and off by clicking the **Apply Filter** button again.

Filter by Form

To filter by form, you just type in the value you are looking for into a blank form. We will look for landlords with the surname **Hemmings**.

——○ Make sure that no filter is currently applied. Click the **Filter By Form** button.

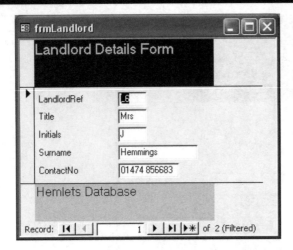

A blank form appears. The **Title** field will probably appear with **Miss** already entered simply because of the previous filter that we applied.

- Clear the query grid either by just deleting the **Miss** entry in the **Title** field or by clicking the **Clear Grid** icon on the toolbar.

- Click in the **Surname** field. Notice that an arrow appears on the right of the field. Click this.

This conveniently gives you a list of all the surnames entered in the database. You can either click a surname in the list or just type it in.

- Click **Hemmings** then click the **Apply Filter** icon.

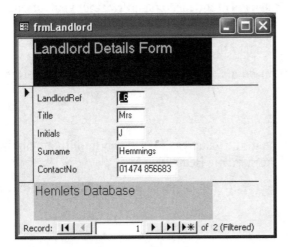

Two records have been filtered. Look at both of them to check they both have the surname **Hemmings**.

- Remove the filter by clicking the **Remove Filter** button.

- Close the **frmLandlord** form to return to the Database window.

Using a filter in a table

This is very similar to using a filter in a form, so we'll just run though this briefly.

◉ Open the **tblLandlord** table in **Datasheet View**.

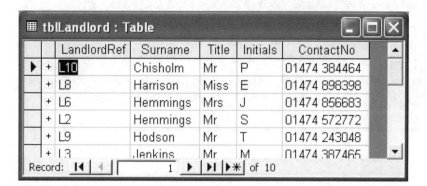

◉ Place the cursor in the **Title** column in a record that says **Miss**.

 ◉ Click the **Filter by Selection** button.

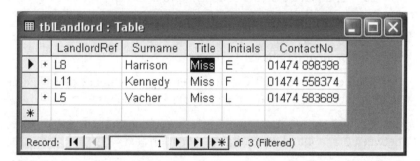

There are three records shown with the title **Miss**.

◉ Remove the filter by clicking the **Remove Filter** button.

 ◉ Now click the **Filter by Form** button.

◉ Clear the grid by clicking the **Clear Grid** button.

◉ Click in the **Surname** field then click the arrow to show the list of surnames.

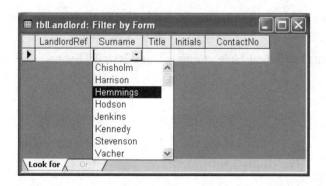

◉ Click **Hemmings**. Click the **Apply Filter** button.

Two records should be displayed with the surname **Hemmings**.

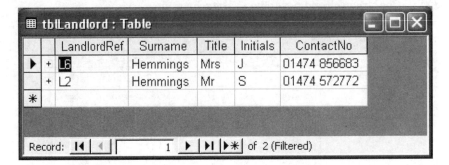

◉ Remove the filter, save and close the table.

Exercise

The **student** database is located on the web site **www.payne-gallway.co.uk/ecdl**. It contains details of about 50 students applying to a college. You need to download **student.mdb** and save it on your own disk. Follow the instructions given on the web site to do this.

1. Open the student database.

2. Add another field named UCAS to the end of the student table. The new field is to be numeric and will hold the student's UCAS points.

3. Set a validation rule for the new field, specifying that the value entered must be between 0 and 480. Enter suitable validation text.

4. Save the table structure.

5. Create a simple form for the **student** table.

6. Save the form as **frmStudent**.

7. Write down the number of records in the database.

8. Find the record for the student whose surname is **Peterson**.

9. Change the name to **Pedersen**.

10. Filter the records to find all the students who come from **Northcliff School**. Write down the first names and surnames of students you found.

11. Filter the records to find all **Male** students from **Eastcliff School**. How many are there?

12. Remove the filter.

13. Save and close the database.

Making Queries

One of the most useful things you can do with a database is to find all the records that satisfy a certain condition, such as "all properties that have 2 bedrooms". Queries are similar to filters, but they allow more scope for changing the format of the results. Queries are useful when you are likely to be searching the database repeatedly for the same thing, because you can easily save them. You can then run the saved query without first opening a table or form.

◉   Load Access and open the **Hemlets** database.

Creating a new query

We'll create a new query that finds all properties that are currently not rented. We can then add other criteria such as number of bedrooms and rent to narrow down the search for a prospective tenant.

◉   In the Database window, select **Queries**.

There are two options, **Create query in Design view** and **Create query by using Wizard**. We'll use the first option.

◉   Double-click **Create query in Design view**.

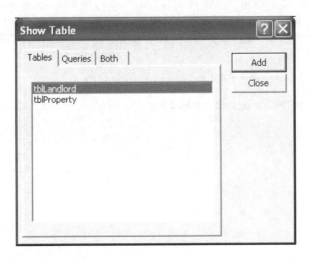

5-69

○ The query will be based on the **tblProperty** table, so click **tblProperty** to select it then click **Add**.

○ Click **Close** to close the **Show Table** window.

The empty query grid appears. Now you need to add fields from the table to the query grid.

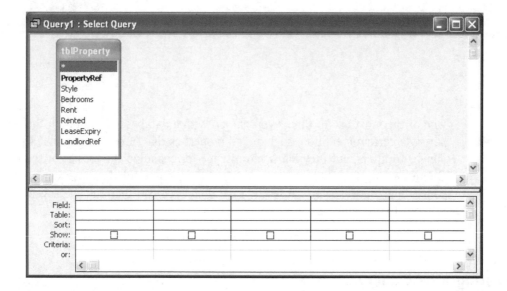

Selecting fields to appear in the query

You need to add a field to the query grid if:

❶ you want to specify a particular value for that field. In our case, we want to specify that the **Rented** field has a **No** value, so **Rented** will have to be put in the grid. We won't actually want to see this field with the results, as we already know that all records selected will not be rented.

❶ you want the field to appear in the results table. You need to show property details like **Style**, **Bedrooms** and **Rent** so that anyone looking through can make a decision on which properties they might be interested in. The **PropertyRef** field should also be included.

○ Double-click the **PropertyRef** field to put it in the grid.

○ Double-click the fields **Style**, **Bedrooms**, **Rent** and **Rented**.

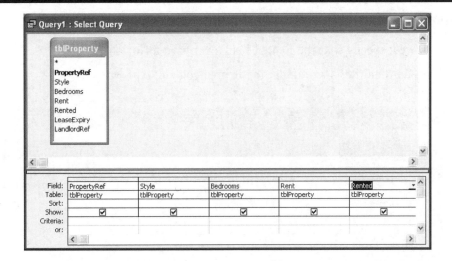

Tip:
You can click and drag a field from the table into the grid if you don't like double-clicking!

Resizing columns

❶ You can change the width of the columns in the query grid so that you can view them all without having to scroll across. Just place the cursor between two column headers so that it changes to a double-headed arrow, then either double-click the mouse or click and drag.

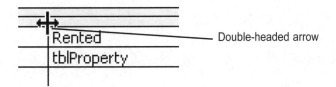

— Double-headed arrow

Removing fields from the grid

◉ Double-click the **LeaseExpiry** field to add it to the query grid.

◉ To delete the **LeaseExpiry** field, click in the column header for the **LeaseExpiry** field then press the **Delete** key.

The column — header

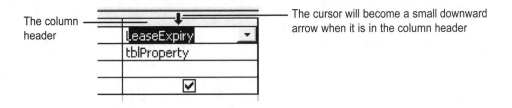

— The cursor will become a small downward arrow when it is in the column header

Adding and removing criteria

Now we'll specify that the **Rented** field must have a **No** value.

◉   In the **Criteria** row under the **Rented** column, type **No**.

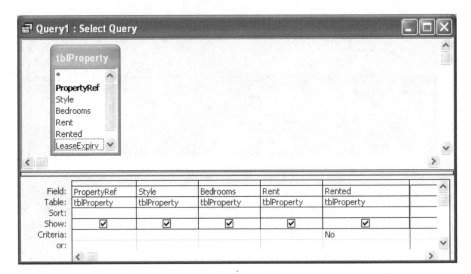

❶   Removing criteria is just as straightforward – just double-click the criteria you want to delete then press the **Backspace** or **Delete** key.

Running the query

◉   Click the **Run** button on the **Query Design** toolbar.

You should get the following Results table.

	PropertyRef	Style	Bedrooms	Rent	Rented
▶	3	Detached	4	£1,050	☐
	5	Semi	3	£850	☐
	7	Flat	1	£500	☐
	8	Flat	2	£600	☐
	10	Semi	3	£900	☐
	11	Semi	3	£775	☐
	13	Semi	2	£750	☐
✱	(AutoNumber)		0	£0	▨

Record: ◀◀ ◀ | 1 | ▶ ▶◀ ▶✱ of 7

You can see that it has successfully selected only those properties that are not currently rented.

It isn't necessary to see the **Rented** column in the Results table because it will always be **No**. We'll hide this column.

Hiding and unhiding fields

We want to hide the **Rented** column.

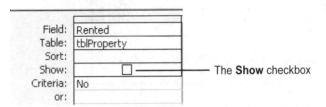

O   Return to **Design View** by clicking the **Design View** icon.

O   Notice that above the **Criteria** row there is a **Show** row. All you need to do to hide a column is to uncheck its **Show** box. Click in the **Show** checkbox in the **Rented** column.

Field:	Rented
Table:	tblProperty
Sort:	
Show:	☐ ———— The **Show** checkbox
Criteria:	No
or:	

O   Run the query again to see that it has worked.

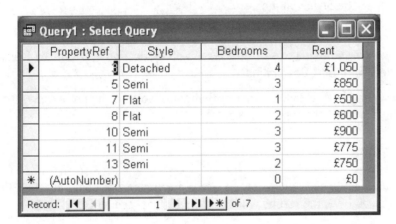

PropertyRef	Style	Bedrooms	Rent
3	Detached	4	£1,050
5	Semi	3	£850
7	Flat	1	£500
8	Flat	2	£600
10	Semi	3	£900
11	Semi	3	£775
13	Semi	2	£750
(AutoNumber)		0	£0

Record: 1 of 7

ⓘ   You can unhide fields simply by clicking the **Show** checkbox again so that it is checked.

Saving the query

Before you do any more, save the query. You will now be able to run this query any time simply by double-clicking its name in the Database window.

O   Click the **Save** icon and enter **qryPropertyForRent** as the query name.

Sorting data in a query output

Data in a table can be sorted in ascending or descending numeric order on any numeric field such as **PropertyRef**, **Bedrooms** or **Rent** in the Query Results table shown above.

O   Click anywhere in the **Rent** column.

O   Click the **Sort Ascending** button.

Now the records appear in this order:

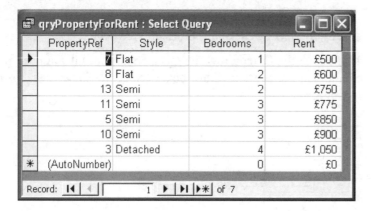

You can also sort in ascending or descending alphabetical order on a text field such as **Style**.

○   Click in the **Style** column.

○   Click the **Sort Ascending** button.

○   Try a different way to sort in reverse alphabetical order. From the **Records** menu select **Sort**, **Sort Descending**.

Now try sorting in Descending order of Bedrooms, so that the properties with the most bedrooms appear at the top of the list.

Sorting on two fields

Sorting the query results table may be useful for a 'one-off' query but next time you run the saved query, the results will be in the original sequence.

You can specify a sort order in the actual query, so that the data will always appear in the desired sequence when you run the query. Also, you can sort on more than one field. (For example, a telephone directory is sorted on **Surname** and then on **Initials**, so that **Smith J.S.** appears before **Smith R.A.**)

In our query, it might be useful if the results were sorted by style and by number of bedrooms. When you want to sort by more than one field, Access has to prioritise which field it will sort by first. Access will sort by the **left-most** field first, so in this query, at the moment the **Style** field is left of **Bedrooms**, so if we sort by both it will sort by **Style** then **Bedrooms**.

○   In **Design View**, click in the **Sort** row of the **Style** column then click the small down-arrow.

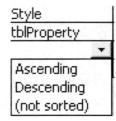

○ Click **Ascending** so that it sorts the house styles alphabetically from A to Z. Note that if you wanted to sort house styles from Z to A (**Semi** before **Flat**), you would select **Descending**.

○ Repeat this for the **Bedrooms** field. Select **Ascending** to sort the properties in order of least to most bedrooms.

○ Run the query.

PropertyRef	Style	Bedrooms	Rent
3	Detached	4	£1,050
7	Flat	1	£500
8	Flat	2	£600
13	Semi	2	£750
11	Semi	3	£775
10	Semi	3	£900
5	Semi	3	£850
(AutoNumber)		0	£0

qryPropertyForRent : Select Query

Record: 1 of 7

That worked – but suppose you wanted to sort first by bedrooms, then house style.

Moving fields

We'll move the **Bedrooms** field to the left of the **Style** field so that Access will sort by bedrooms first.

○ Return to **Design View**.

○ Click the column header for the **Bedrooms** column so that the whole column is selected.

○ Click and drag the column to the left of the **Style** field. When you are dragging, you can tell where the column will be dropped by a black line between the columns. Release the mouse when the black line is to the left of the **Style** field (see below).

Field:	PropertyRef	Style	Bedrooms	Rent	Rented	
Table:	tblProperty	tblProperty	tblProperty	tblProperty	tblProperty	
Sort:		Ascending	Ascending			
Show:	☑	☑	☑	☑	☐	☐
Criteria:					No	
or:						

O Run the query to see if it has worked!

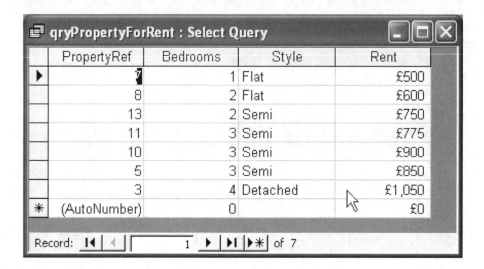

Adding a second table to the query

If you wanted to see who the landlord was for each of these properties, you would have to add the **tblLandlord** table to the query.

O Return to **Design View**.

 O Click the **Show Table** button on the **Query Design** toolbar.

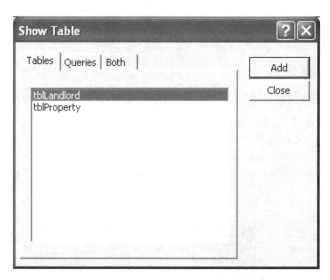

O Make sure **tblLandlord** is selected then click **Add**. Click **Close**.

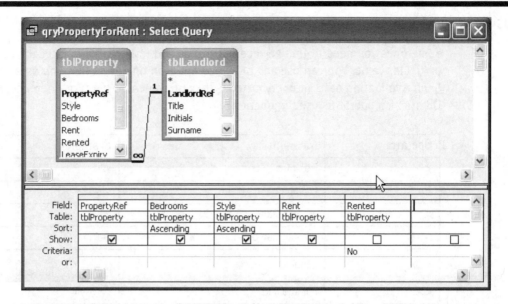

tblLandlord is added to the query. Now we want to add the fields **Title**, **Initials** and **Surname** from the **tblLandlord** table to the query grid.

- Double-click the fields **Title**, **Initials** and **Surname** from **tblLandlord** to add them.

- Run the query.

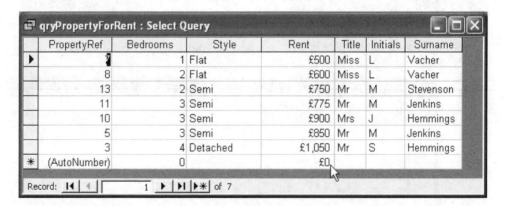

Now you can see who owns which property!

Tip:

If you get lots of repeated rows, just check you haven't added any of the tables more than once. Do this by using the scroll bars in the top part of the query window in Design View to search for extra tables.

Using operators

Sometimes you need to find all records with a field less than or greater than a particular value. You can use any of the **comparison operators** that you used in Chapter 5.5 for validating data, in query criteria. They are repeated here for reference. **AND** and **OR** are also operators used in queries.

Operator	Meaning	Example
<	less than	<20
<=	less than or equal to	<=20
>	greater than	>0
>=	greater than or equal to	>=0
=	equal to	=20 ="Flat" OR "Terraced"
<>	not equal to	<>"Semi"
BETWEEN	test for a range of values. Must be two comparison values (a low & high value) separated by AND operator	BETWEEN 01/12/2002 AND 25/12/2002
AND	All criteria must be satisfied	Bedrooms>1 AND Rent<800 AND Rented="No"
OR	At least one of the criteria must be satisfied	="Flat" OR "Semi"

Add some more criteria to your query so that it looks like the one below:

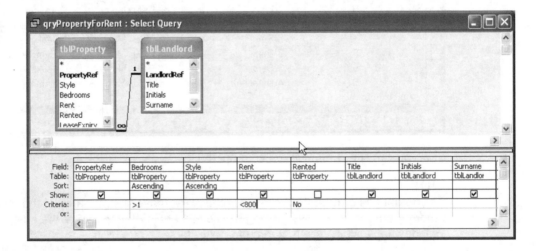

◉ Run the query to see the effect of the criteria.

qryPropertyForRent : Select Query						
PropertyRef	Bedrooms	Style	Rent	Title	Initials	Surname
▶ 3	2	Flat	£600	Miss	L	Vacher
13	2	Semi	£750	Mr	M	Stevenson
11	3	Semi	£775	Mr	M	Jenkins
* (AutoNumber)	0		£0			

Record: ◀◀ ◀ | 1 | ▶ ▶▶ ▶* of 3

◉ Save your query.

Notice that when you set query criteria, criteria placed on the same line ALL have to be satisfied. This is equivalent to the "AND" condition in the Operator table above.

To enter criteria to find all properties which are EITHER "Flat" OR "Semi", you could write the criteria as shown below:

PropertyRef	Bedrooms	Style	Rent	Title	In
tblProperty	tblProperty	tblProperty	tblProperty	tblLandlord	tb
	Ascending	Ascending			
☑	☑	☑	☑	☑	
		"Flat" Or "Semi"			

Alternatively, you can write the criteria one beneath the other:

PropertyRef	Bedrooms	Style	Rent	Title	In
tblProperty	tblProperty	tblProperty	tblProperty	tblLandlord	tb
	Ascending	Ascending			
☑	☑	☑	☑	☑	
		"Flat"			
		"Semi"			

You could find all properties which are EITHER 1-bedroomed OR a Flat:

PropertyRef	Bedrooms	Style	Rent	Title	In
tblProperty	tblProperty	tblProperty	tblProperty	tblLandlord	tb
	Ascending	Ascending			
☑	☑	☑	☑	☑	
		"Flat"			
	1				

This produces the following results table:

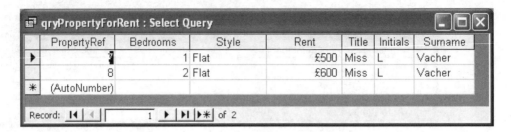

Printing a query

All the options for printing a query are very similar to those for printing a table or form.

○ In **Datasheet View** (the Results table), click the **Print Preview** icon.

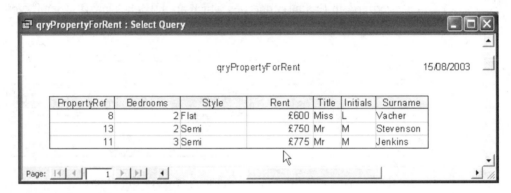

○ Click **Close** to exit **Print Preview**.

○ Select **File**, **Page Setup** then click the **Page** tab to change page orientation and paper size.

○ Select **File**, **Print** to set which pages to print and the number of copies. If you want to print, click **OK**, otherwise click **Cancel**.

○ Close the query by clicking the **Close** button.

Tip:

In the Database window, you will see your query when the **Queries** tab is selected. You can delete an unwanted query by selecting it and pressing the **Delete** key.

Exercise

1. (a) Open the **student** database that you downloaded from the web site **www.payne-gallway.co.uk/ecdl**.

    (b) Create a query to select all records of students who come from Westcliff School. Display only the fields for **Surname**, **Forename**, **Sex** and **School**.

    (c) Run the query.

    (d) Sort the records in the results table so that all the records for male students appear before all female students.

    (e) Save your query as **qryWestcliff**.

    (f) Print the query results.

2. (a) Create a second query to select all records of students who were born before 01/09/1986.

    (b) Sort the records into ascending order of Surname and Forename.

    (c) Save your query as **qryStudentAge**

    (d) Run the query.

    (e) Print out the query results on a single page in Landscape orientation.

5.10 Reports

Suppose you want to present the data in a table or query in a neater way, for example with a proper title. For this you would use a Report. Reports allow you to present data in a wide variety of ways. They can be based on queries or on tables.

○ Make sure the **Hemlets** database is open and you can see the Database window.

Reports based on tables

First we'll create a report based on the **tblLandlord** table which will simply list all the landlords and their contact details.

○ In the Database window, click to select the **Reports** tab.

○ Double-click **Create report by using wizard**.

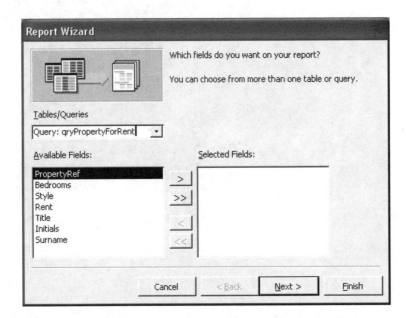

○ Select **tblLandlord** from the **Tables/Queries** dropdown list.

○ We want all the fields to appear in the report, so click **>>**. Click **Next**.

○ You are asked about **Grouping Levels**. We won't need any for this report, so leave the settings as below:

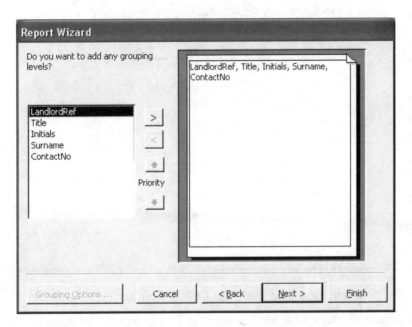

○ Click **Next**. We can specify a sort order. It would be useful to have the landlords sorted by **Surname**, so select **Surname** from the first dropdown list and leave the button adjacent as **Ascending**. Click **Next**.

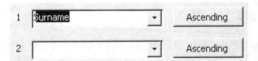

○ Click **Next** two more times – you don't need to make changes to the presentation.

○ Give the report the title **rptLandlordDetails**. This is what the report will then be saved as.

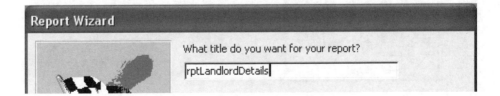

Tip:
Although Access only asks you for a title for the report, it will actually save the report with the title name.

○ Click **Finish** to view the report.

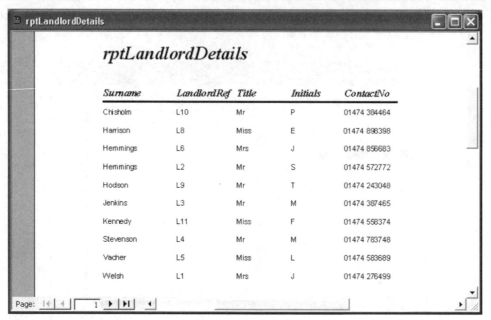

 Go to **Design View** by clicking the **Design View** icon.

Now we'll change the title of the report. First click where it says **rptLandlordDetails** so that handles appear around the title, and then click again on the title text. Now you can delete the text and type the new title, **Landlord Details**.

Adding text to Headers and Footers

 The Toolbox should be visible on your screen. If it is not, click the Toolbox icon.

There is already some text in the **Report Header** – the title. We'll add another label.

Click the **Label** icon, then click and drag out a rectangle to the right of the title.

Type the text **Hemlets Ltd**.

Now we'll do the same with the **Report Footer**.

○ Click the **Label** icon, then click and drag out a rectangle at the bottom of the report under the **Report Footer**. Don't worry that there's no page there yet.

○ Type the text **Hemlets Database**.

Your report should look something like this:

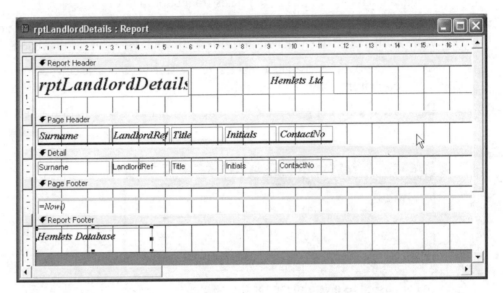

You can modify the footer text by clicking in the box and editing it.

○ View the report by clicking the **Print Preview** icon.

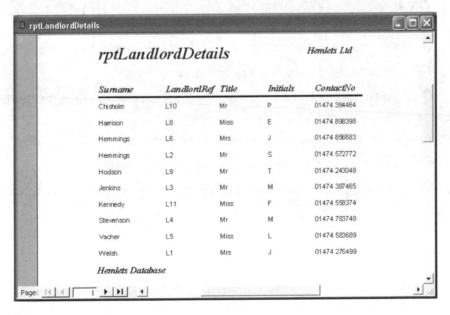

○ Save and close your report.

Reports based on queries

Hemlets would like a report that lists each landlord and the properties they own that are being rented out. Hemlets will use this to calculate how much rent the landlord is earning every month.

This report will use data from both **tblLandlord** and **tblProperty**, and will use as its source a query that combines the fields from both tables.

We already have a query that contains the fields we want – the **qryPropertyForRent**. We will copy the query then change the criteria to what we need for the report.

○   In the Database window, make sure the **Queries** tab is selected, then click **qryPropertyForRent** to select it.

○   Select **Edit**, **Copy** from the menu at the top of the screen. Now select **Edit**, **Paste** from the menu.

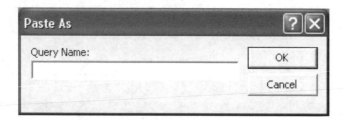

You are asked to give a name for the new query.

○   Type **qryLandlordIncome** and click **OK**.

Tip:
You can copy and paste all other database objects like **Tables** and **Forms** in just the same way.

   ○   Now open **qryLandlordIncome** in **Design View** by selecting it then clicking **Design**.

We'll delete all the criteria currently in the query grid.

○   Delete each criterion in turn by clicking it, then using either the **Delete** or **Backspace** keys.

We also want to remove all the entries in the **Sort** row.

○   Delete these in the same way as you did the **Criteria**.

○   Add the criterion **Yes** to the **Rented** column. Your query should now look like the one on the next page.

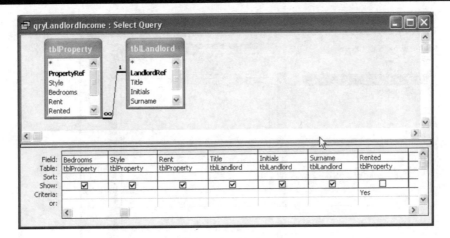

○ It is a good idea to add the sorting rules in the query rather than the report. Move the **Surname** field to the left of the query and give it an **Ascending** sort. This will sort the landlords alphabetically in the query.

○ Give the **Rent** column a **Descending** sort.

○ Save and close the query.

Creating the report

○ In the Database window, click to select the **Reports** tab.

○ Double-click **Create report by using wizard**.

○ Make sure **qryLandlordIncome** is selected in the **Tables/Queries** box. We want all the fields in the query except **Style** and **Bedrooms**. To include a field, just click to select it, then click >.

○ Click the fields in the order shown.

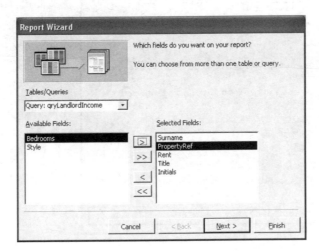

○ Click **Next**. You are now asked how you want to view the data. We want the results grouped by **Landlord**, so click to select **tblLandlord**.

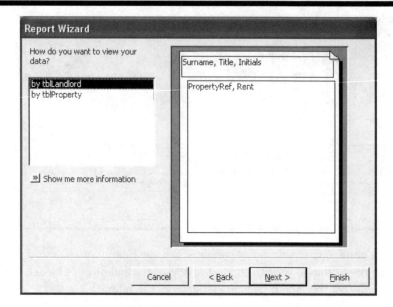

- Click **Next**. We don't need to add any grouping levels, as the results are already grouped by **tblLandlord**, so just click **Next**.

- You can now specify which fields you want to sort by. We've already set the sorting rules in the underlying query so we don't need to specify them again here. Click **Next**.

- Click **Next** two more times – you don't need to change any of the presentation options.

- Give the report the title **rptLandlordIncome**; this is what it will be saved as.

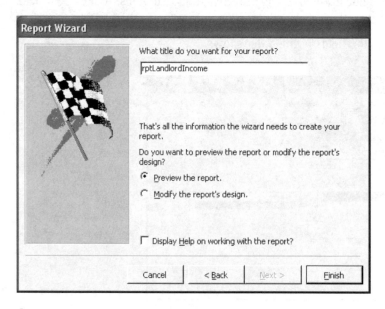

- Click **Finish**.

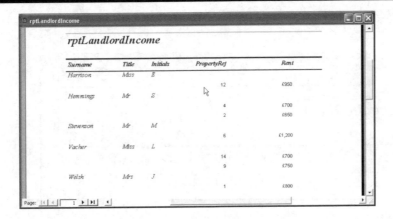

Your report will appear!

We've got a few changes and additions to make to it, which we'll do in **Design View**.

 ●   Change to **Design View** by clicking the **Design View** icon.

Adding a Sum field

We need the report to calculate the total income for each landlord by summing the rent for each of the properties that are rented.

To sum the rent for each landlord separately, we need to add a field to the **Group Footer**. Currently there is no **Group Footer** so we'll add it now.

●   Click the **Sorting and Grouping** button on the **Report Design** toolbar.

Notice that the report is sorted in Ascending order of Surname (A–Z). You could change this by clicking next to the word **Ascending** and selecting **Descending** from the dropdown menu.

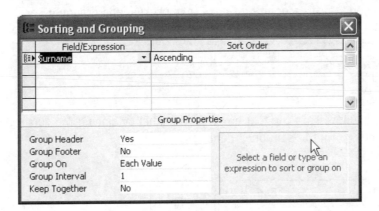

●   At the bottom where it says **Group Footer**, change the **No** to a **Yes**.

●   Close the **Sorting and Grouping** window by clicking its red **Close** icon.

There should now be a section on the report called **Surname Footer**.

●   Now we'll add a field. Click the **Text Box** button in the toolbox.

○ Click once in the **Surname Footer** to insert the field.

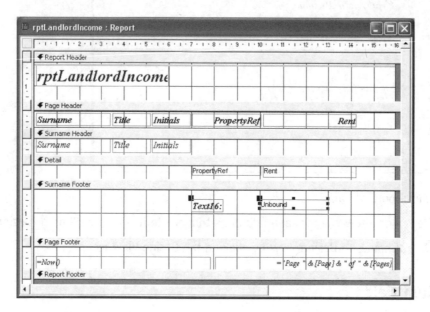

○ Click where it says **Unbound**, and change the text to say **=Sum(Rent)**.

○ Change the label from **Text16** to **Total Rental Income**.

○ Right-justify the **Rent** label and field by selecting the field then clicking the **Align Right** button.

○ Now we'll change the title to say **Landlord Income Report**. Click where it says **rptLandlordIncome** so that handles appear around the title, then click again on the title text. Now you can delete the text and type the new title.

❸ You can move the fields individually by placing the cursor in the top left-hand corner so that it's a pointing finger, then clicking and dragging.

❸ You can move both the text box with the label by placing the cursor over the text box so that it is an open hand.

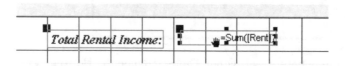

❸ You can make the **Surname Footer** bigger or smaller by clicking and dragging the grey border between sections.

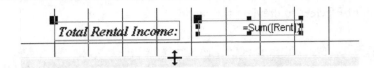

❶ You can resize the text boxes by clicking and dragging the handles that appear when you select them.

▶ Reposition the fields to look like the report below:

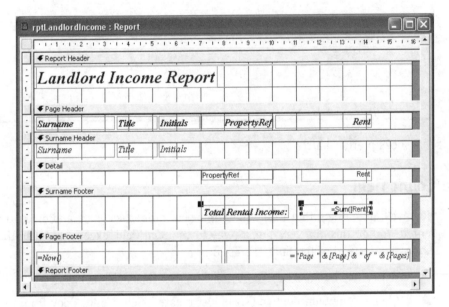

▶ Right-click the **field =Sum(Rent)** and select **Properties** in the pop-up menu.

▶ In the Properties box, change the **Format** to **Currency**, and **Decimal Places** to **0**.

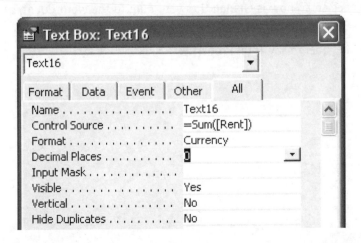

◯ Click **Print Preview** to preview the report.

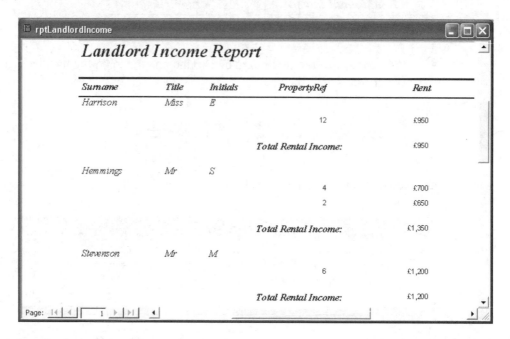

That looks pretty smart!

Adding a Count field

Now we'll add a field that totals the number of properties each landlord currently has rented. You do this in a very similar way to the **Sum** field, except we'll use the **Count** expression instead of the **Sum** expression.

 ◯ Return to the report design by clicking the **Design View** icon.

◯ Click on the **Sum** field you have just created. Select **Edit, Copy** from the menu.

◯ Now select **Edit, Paste** from the menu. The field will be copied and pasted below the original.

◯ All you need to do now is change the word **Sum** to the word **Count**, as shown below.

◯ Change the label to say **Total Properties:**.

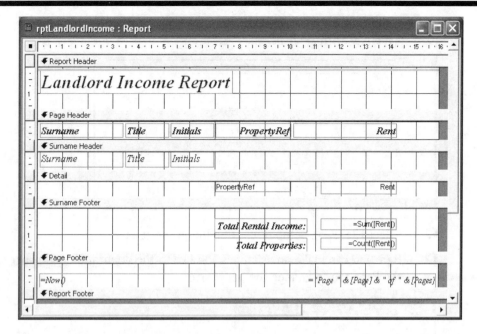

- ● In the Properties box, change the Format property to **General Number**, and **Decimal Places** to **0**.

- ● Preview the report by clicking **Print Preview**.

Other useful expressions

So far you've used the **Sum** and **Count** expressions. Others which you can also substitute in are:

- ❶ **Minimum**: gives the minimum value of all values in the group. In our example, where there was more than one property it would give the value of the smallest rent.

- ❶ **Maximum**: like minimum, except gives the maximum rent for a particular landlord's properties.

- ❶ **Average**: gives the average of all values in the group. In our example where there is more than one property, it would give the average of all the rents for each landlord.

Printing a report

This is very similar to printing tables, forms and queries.

You are already familiar with the report **Print Preview**.

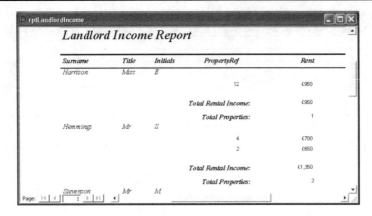

●   Select **File**, **Page Setup** or click **Setup** on the toolbar.

●   Here you can make any changes you like to the orientation and paper size. Click the **Page** tab to change the paper size.

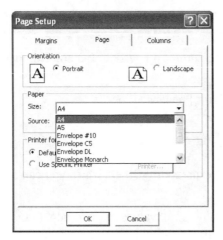

●   Select **File**, **Print** from the menu.

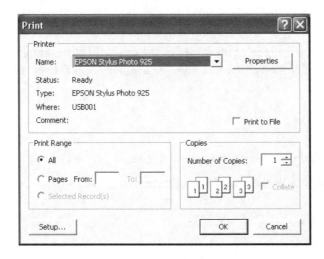

Here you can select which pages of the report to print and how many copies you want.

○ Click **OK** to print, otherwise click **Cancel**.

 ○ Save and close the report, either by clicking the **Close** icon or by selecting **File**, **Close** from the menu bar. Click **Yes** when asked if you wish to save your changes.

Tip:
You can delete an unwanted report by selecting it in the Database window and pressing the **Delete** key.

○ Close the database. You've reached the end of the module!

Exercise

The **Softball** database, which you should download from the Payne-Gallway web site **www.payne-gallway.co.uk/ecdl**, contains information on players and teams in a Softball league. The database contains two tables, a **Team** table for team information such as coach name and contact number, and a **Player** table containing data on the players in each team, such as surname and position.

1.   Open the **Softball** database.

2.   Create a query using both tables and all fields.

3.   Save the query as **query1**.

4.   Create a report based on **query1**. Group the report by **TeamName**; sort the results by **Surname**.

5.   Save the report as **report1**.

6.   Add a **Count** field to count the players in each team.

7.   Save and close the database.

Index — Database